AGELESS INDIA - 1

SHRAMANA'S VIEW OF INDIAN HISTORY

Drawings by Premola Ghose

Series Editor
MALVIKA SINGH

LIMITED
EDITIONS

AN IMPRINT OF
ACADEMIC FOUNDATION

INTRODUCTION TO THE SERIES

This series of Notebooks was conceived as a vibrant and energetic representation of India, manifesting images of her past and present, her remarkable and infinite civilisation with its endless layers of diversity merging and melding into one another, creating a fabric of seamless transitions laced with overlaps of buoyant contradictions that are often unpredictable and mysterious, allowing for flights of the imagination, and leaving 'room for wonder'.

Through the pages of *Ageless India*, this extraordinary and finely nuanced, ever-evolving and contemporary destination on earth, continues to draw into its complex unstitched folds, the many stories and experiences, the influences and ideas that emerge from a 'planet', continually revolving ecliptically on its firm axis, sharing experience and endorsing a sublime unity in exciting and invigorating diversity.

The voyeur in us can use these books to exchange notes, share ideas, articulate intangible reflections in words, and more, to leave them as 'memories' that can be savoured today, as well as in the years to come, by family and friends, to keep the connect of the past with the future alive.

Ageless India will showcase the personalised 'India' of men and women impassioned by her many 'plots' and 'sub-plots', using the skill of their hands and eyes to capture for posterity, her changing avatars, her multiple expressions. The series will be infinite...

Malvika Singh
New Delhi 2015

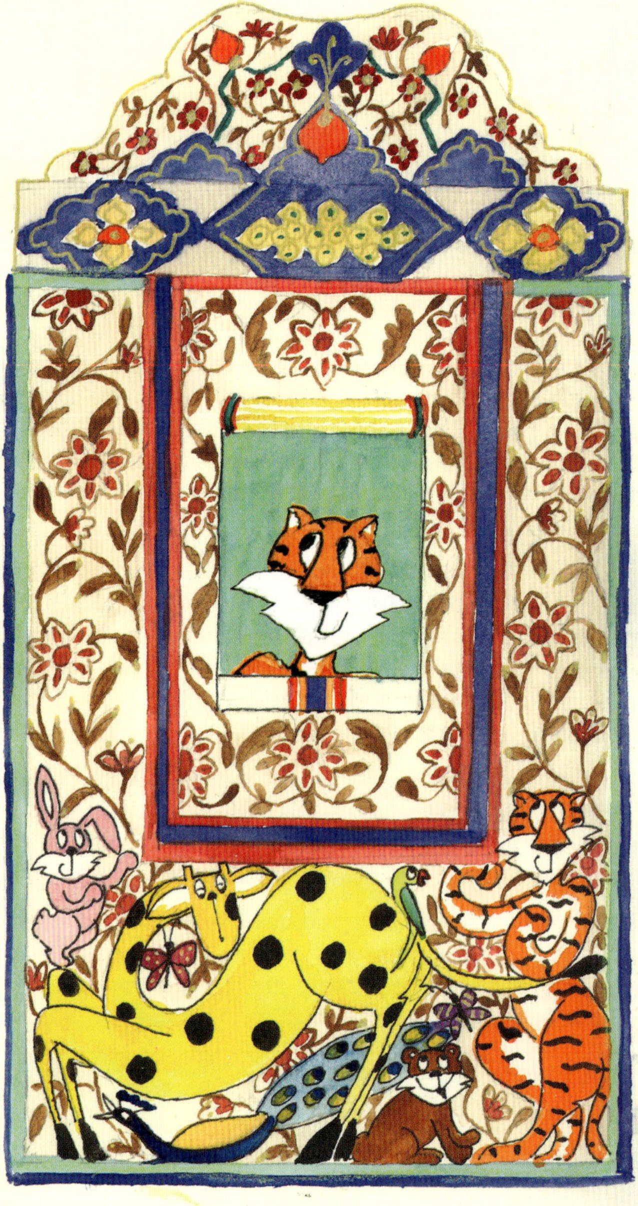

AGELESS INDIA - 1

SHRAMANA'S VIEW OF INDIAN HISTORY

This is the first edition of a series: AGELESS INDIA with enchanting, ethereal images of a land that is often mysterious, its layered histories enticing the senses, creating room for wonder, all merging seamlessly with the vitality and assertive energy of the present. Rarely do past centuries jostle and fight for space with the contemporary, as in India. Write your private stories in these books as you traverse the past and the present of an unusual civilisation, to later share the experiences with those you love and cherish.

Series Editor
MALVIKA SINGH

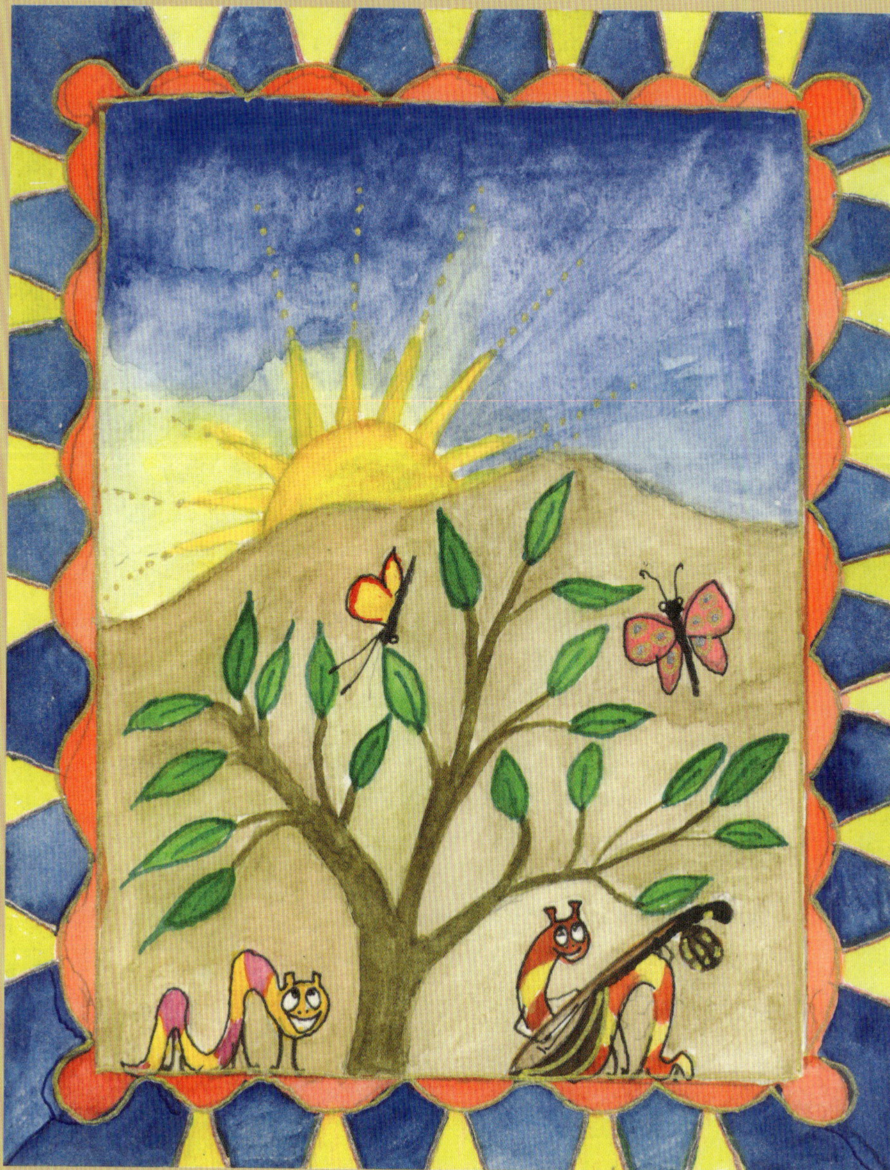

Dawn over Jambudwipa, the land of the wood-apple trees and the ancient name for the Indian subcontinent, in some remote and mythical times.

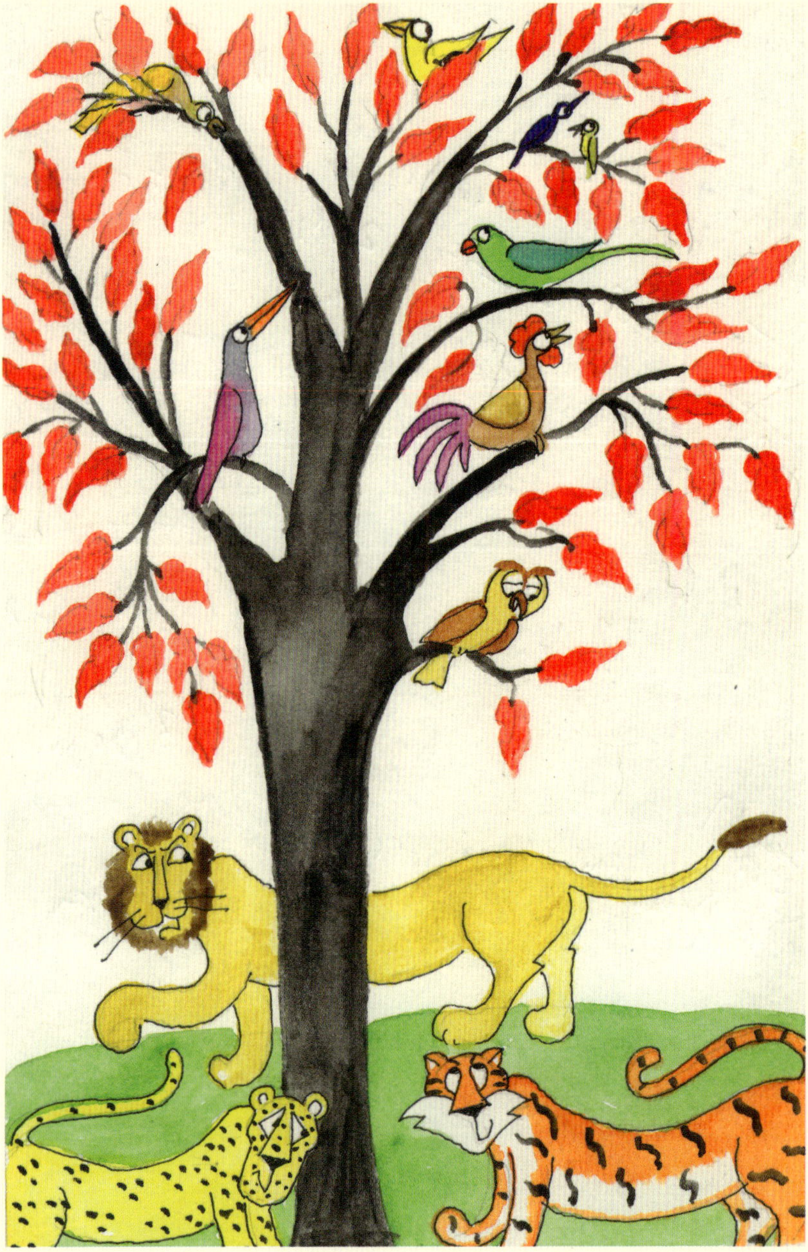

Evolution: The jungle came first, but naturally...Inevitably, the hunter-gatherers followed close on their heels. Peace disappeared.

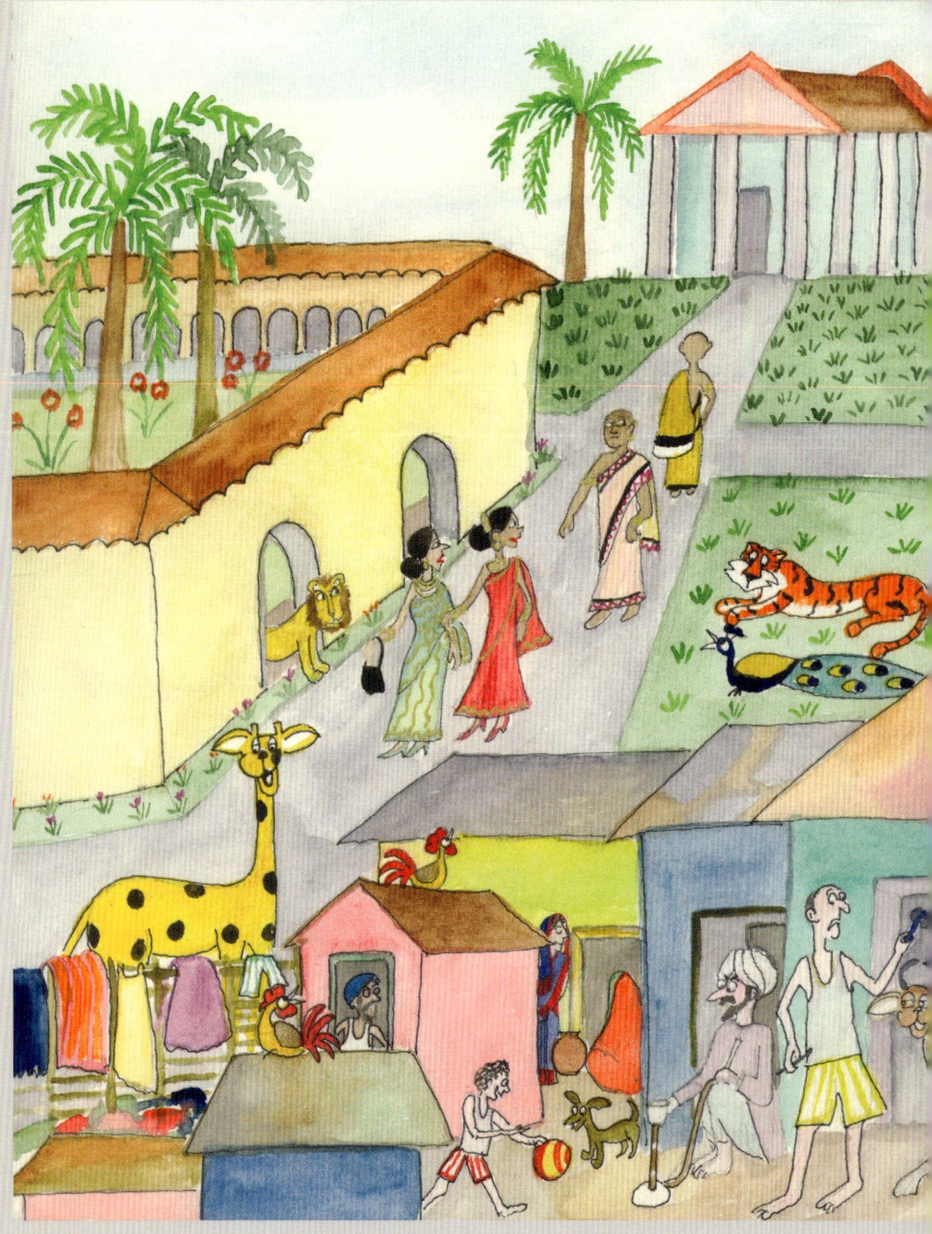

2900-1900 BC, Controversies Galore: Indus Valley Civilisation and the resident Aryans of India. Many scholars believe that the Aryan homeland was in India, so here they are in their natural habitat.

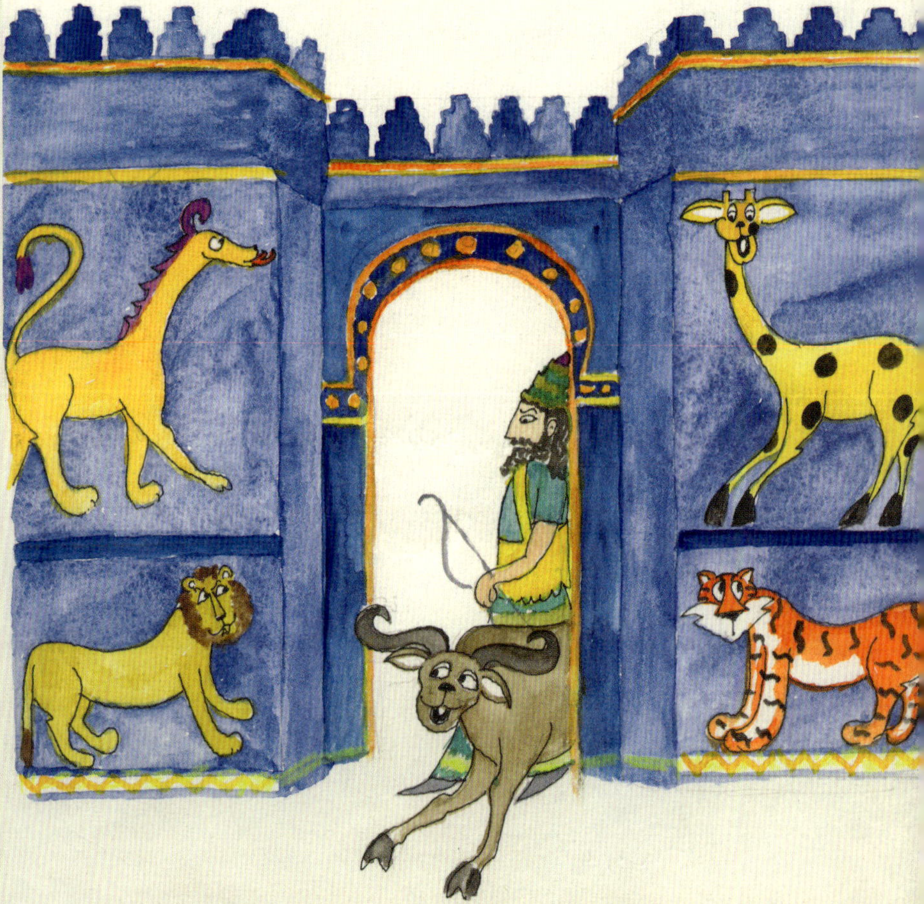

Trade between India and the Middle East: The Indian tiger, the first export, seen on Babylon's Ishtar Gate.

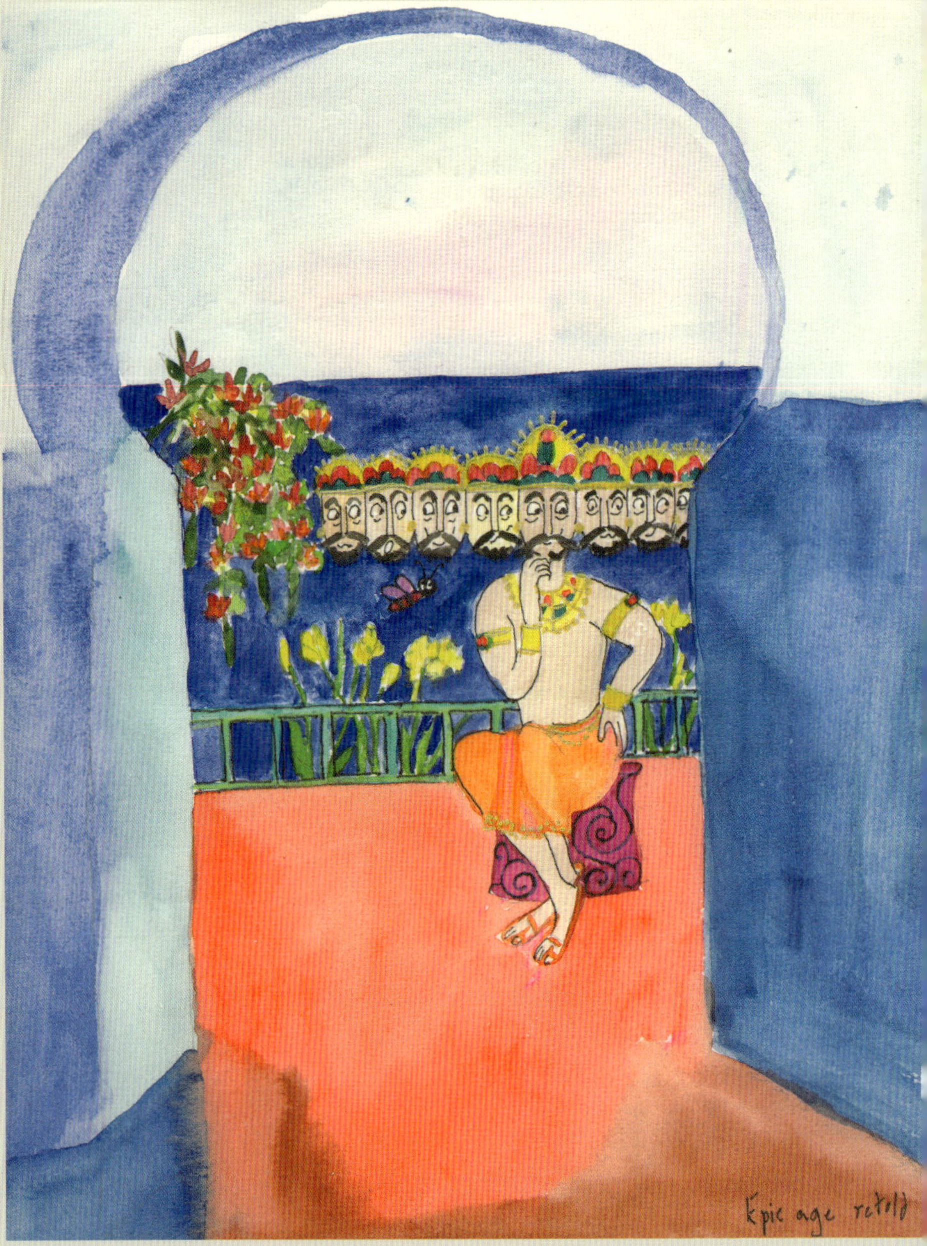
Epic age retold

The Age of the Epics: Ramayana:
The demon king of Lanka, Ravana musing on the beauty of the captive Sita, in his garden overlooking the Indian Ocean.

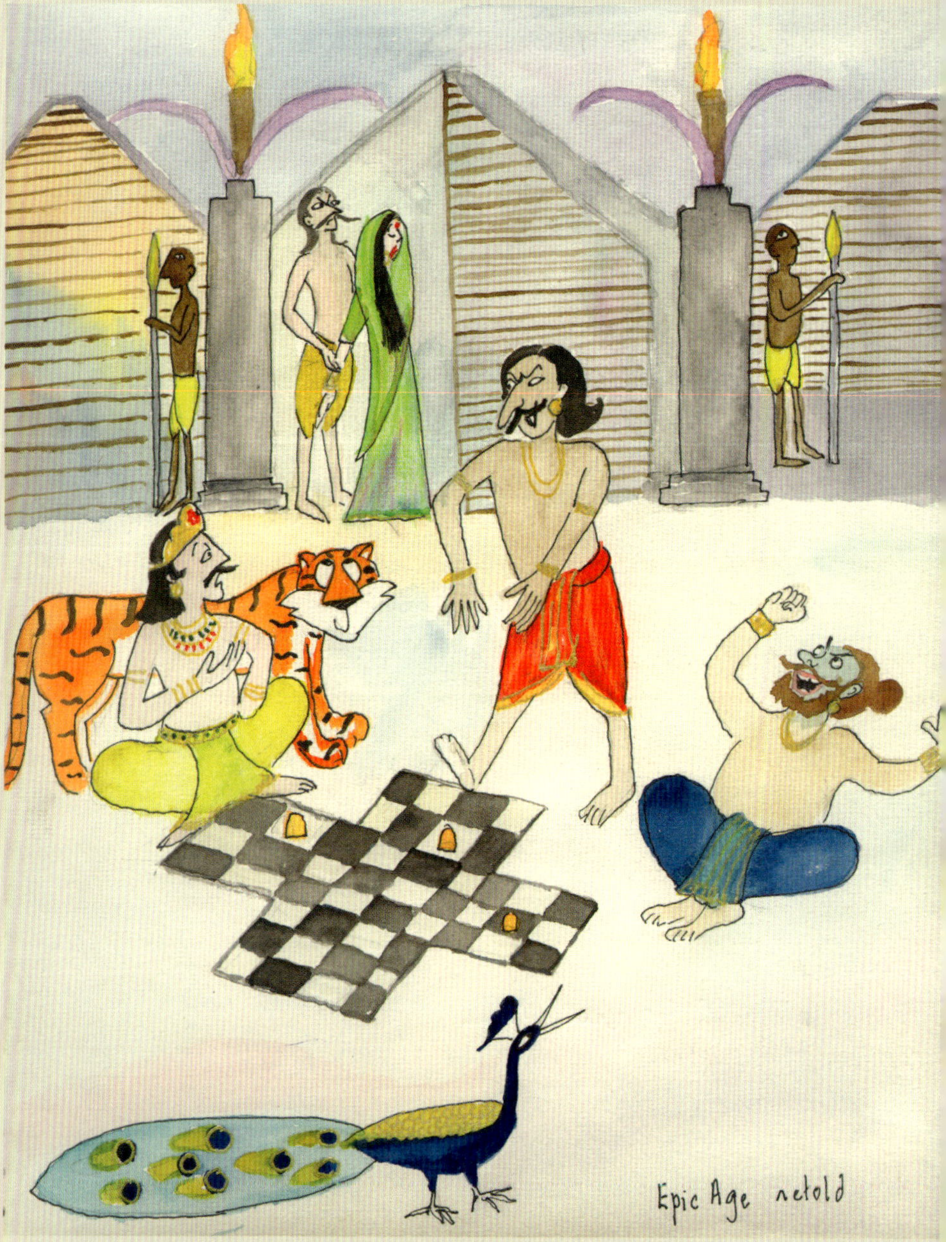
Epic Age retold

The Age of the Epics: The Great War of the Mahabharata: Here is the prelude to war, the game of dice.

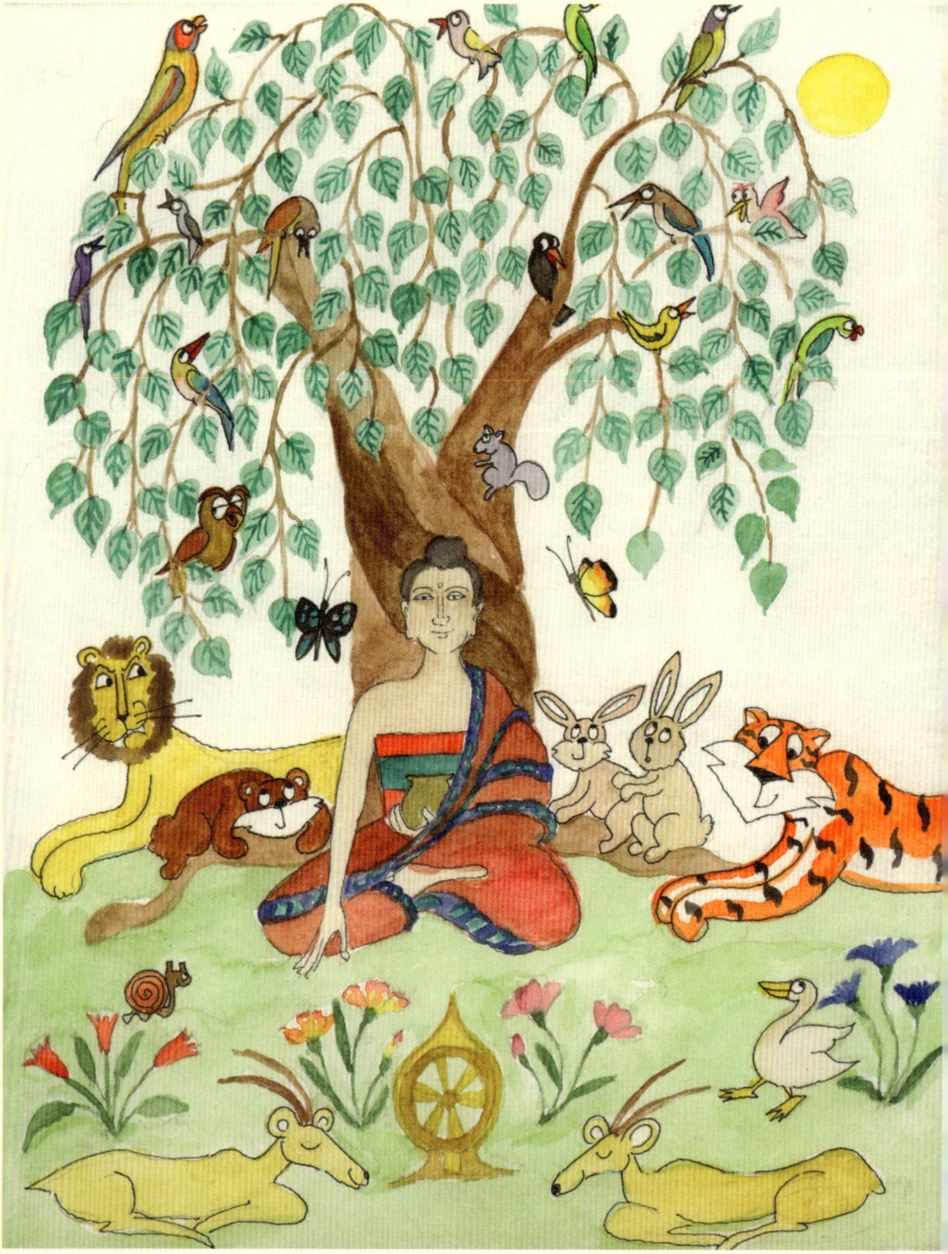

Gautama Buddha (563-483 BC) attains Enlightenment under the Bodhi Tree and in fine company. When he got up, he strolled to Benaras to teach anyone and everyone about the Four Noble Truths of Buddhism.

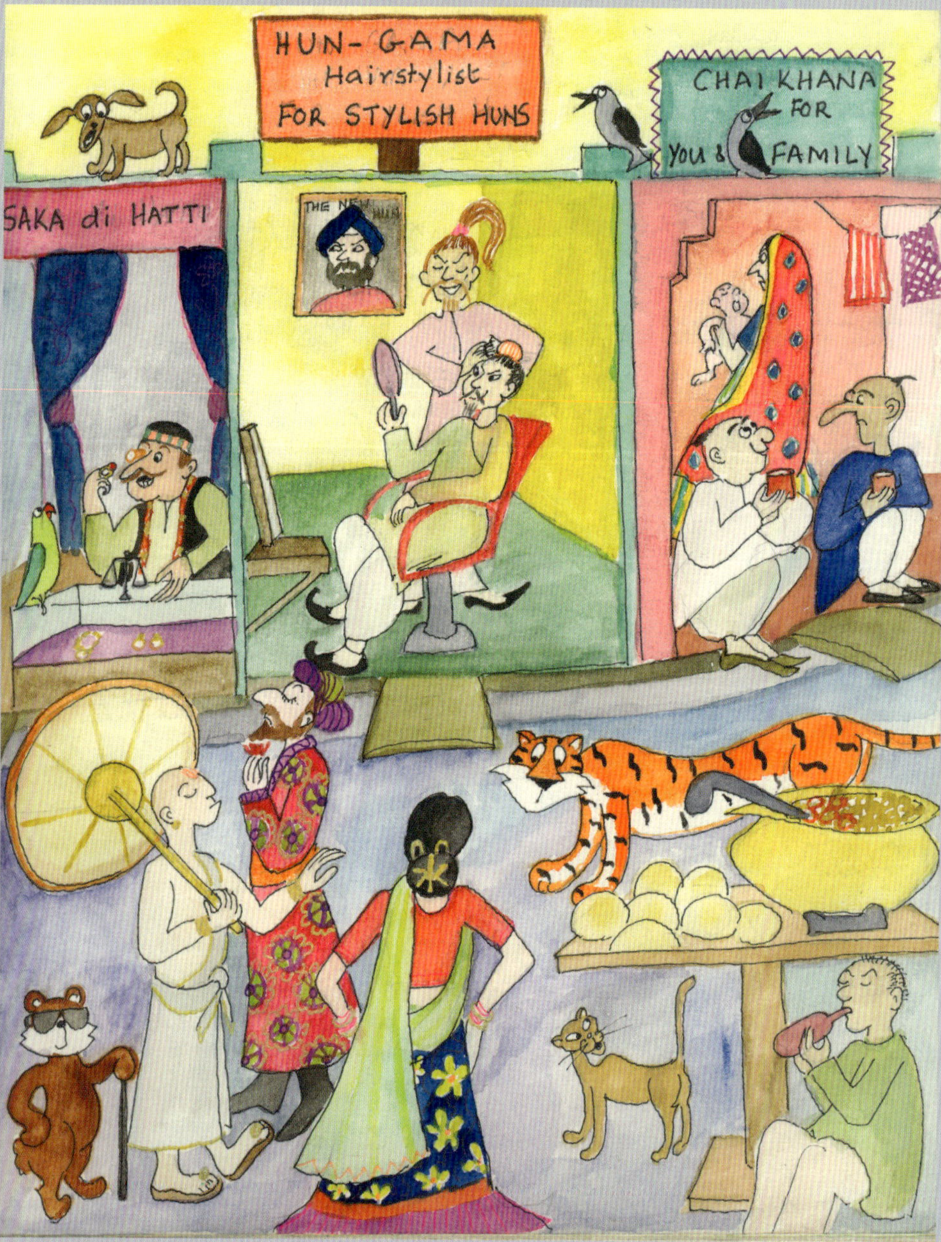
HUN-GAMA
Hairstylist
FOR STYLISH HUNS
CHAI KHANA
FOR
YOU & FAMILY
SAKA di HATTI
THE NEW HUN

350 BC, Taxila, the great and cosmopolitan Asian hub, before Alexander of Macedon's invasion and the first evidence of *chhole-bhature* (spicy chickpeas and native bread) which became the national dish of the region.

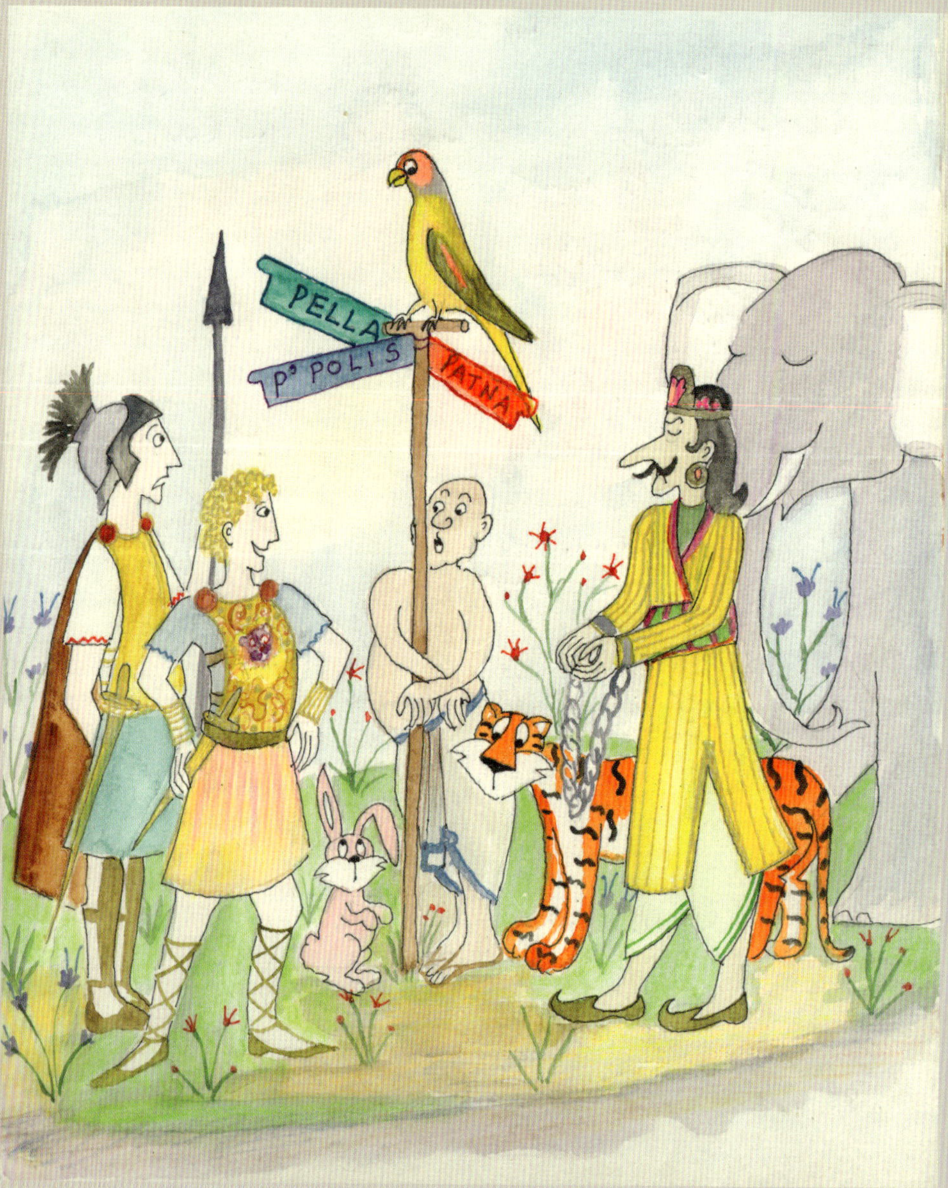
PELLA
P'POLIS
PATNA

326 BC: "Treat me like a King" said the defeated Porus to Alexander. Alexander defeated the Indian raja, Porus, at the terrible battle of Hydaspes and he is said to have uttered these noble words when he was brought to Alexander.

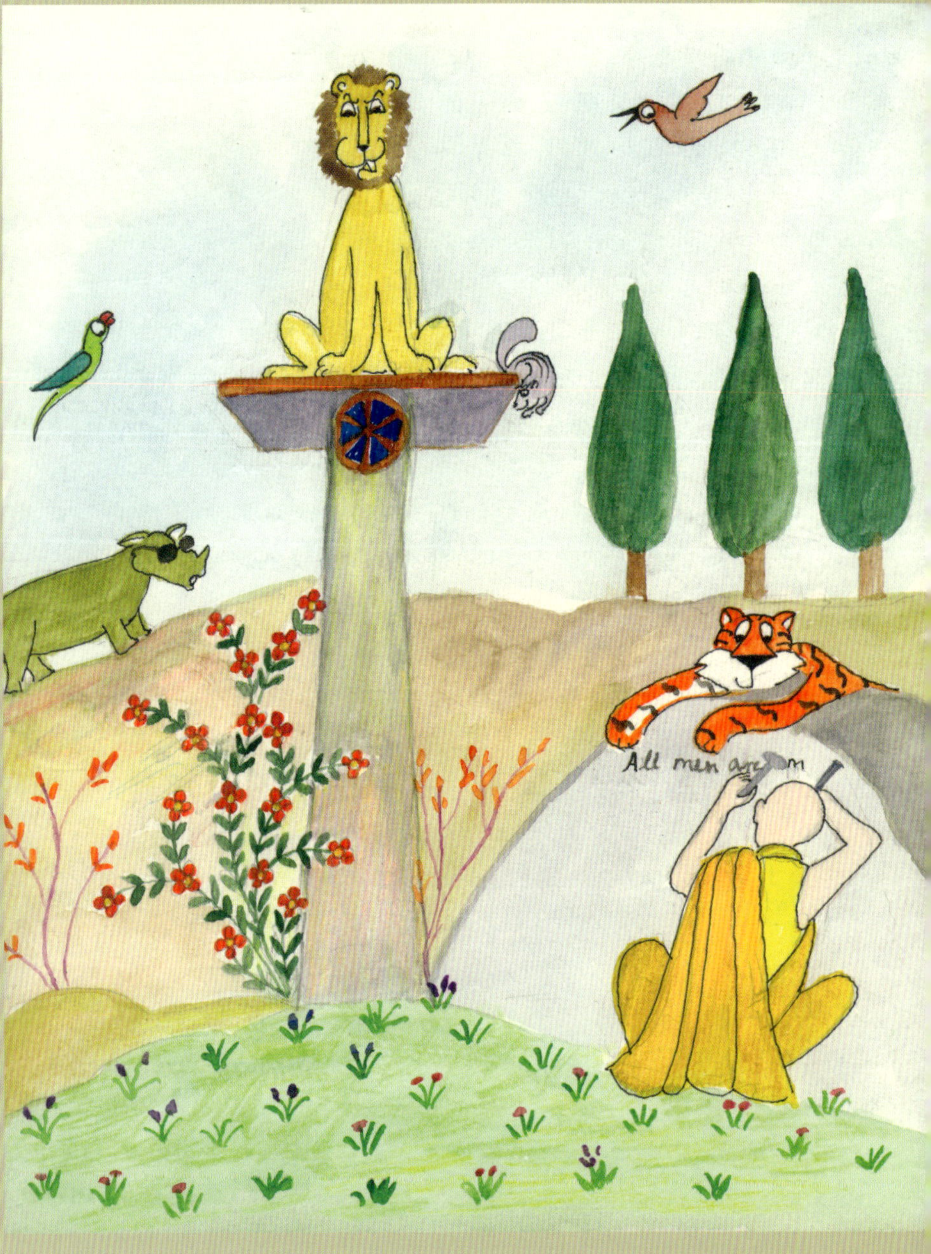
All men

261 BC: The Mauryan emperor Ashoka's remorse after the slaughter at Kalinga and thus he carved on every rock, "all men are my brothers". It is said that Ashoka converted to Buddhism then and there and soon after began to carve lots of his virtuous thoughts on every rock and pillar he could find.

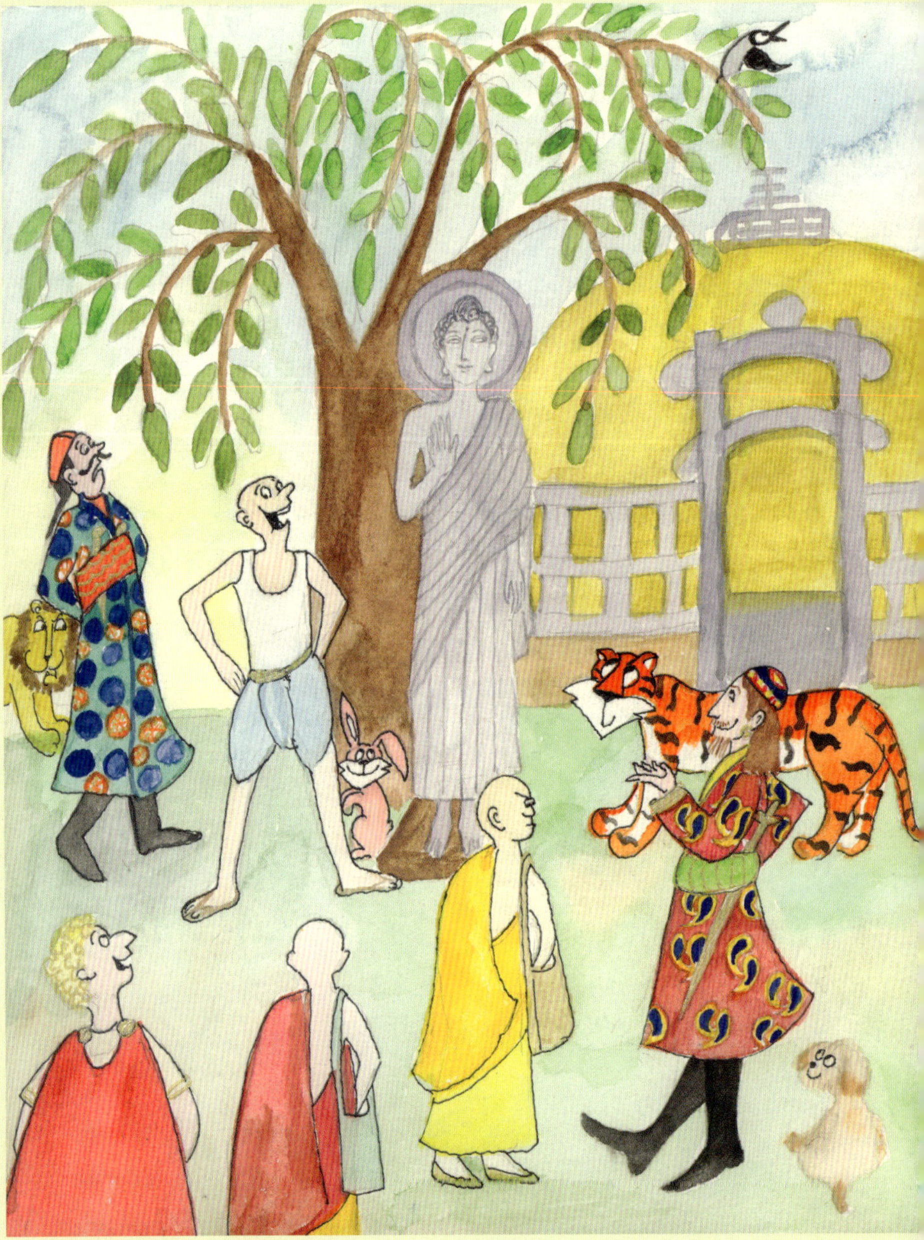

Sometime during the reign of the Kushan emperor Kaniskha (127-140 AD), an unknown sculptor made a statue of the Buddha. Before that, the Buddha was represented by feet, or a tree or even an umbrella. This same statue has been copied for two thousand years. Go anywhere in Asia and you will find 'em!

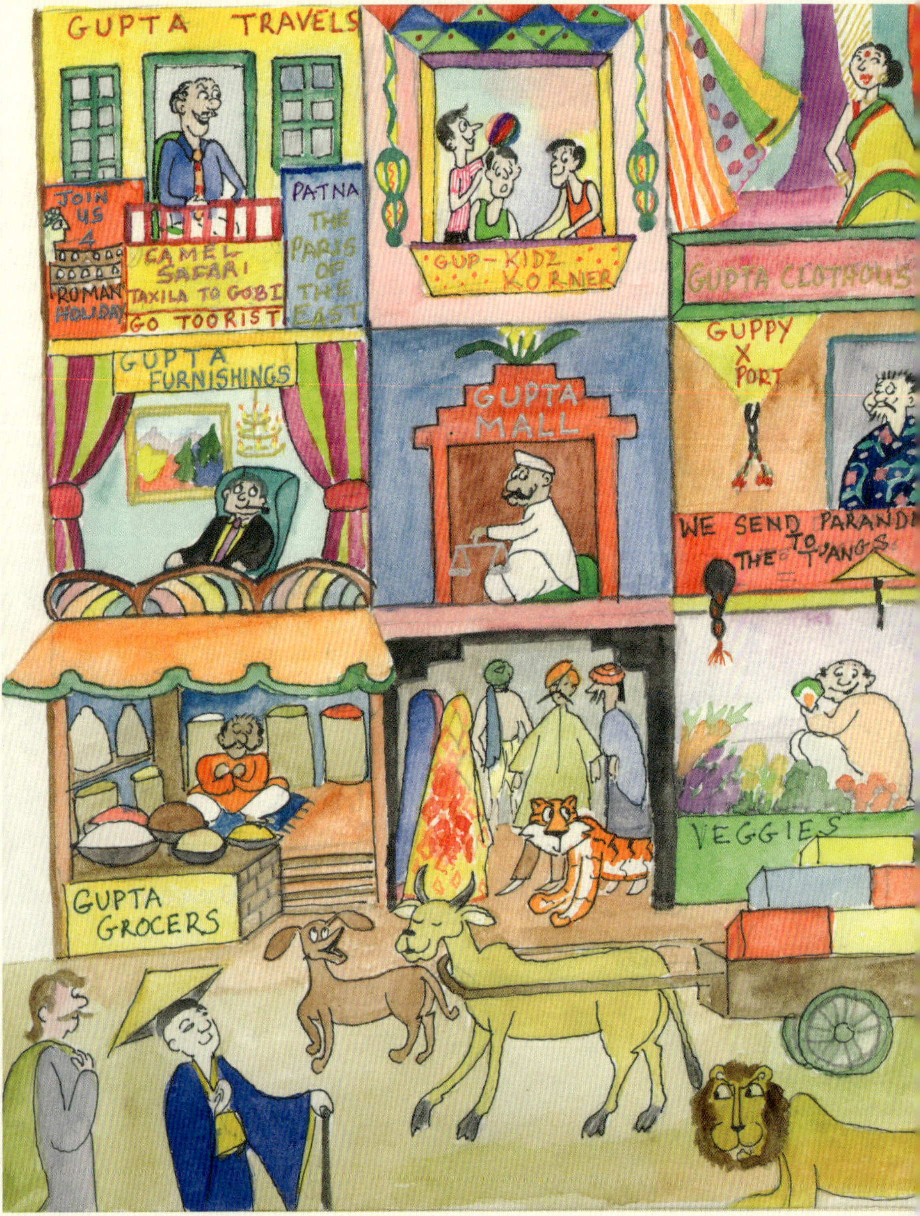
GUPTA TRAVELS
JOIN US 4 ROMAN HOLIDAY
CAMEL SAFARI
TAXILA TO GOBI
GO TOORIST
PATNA THE PARIS OF THE EAST
GUP-KIDZ KORNER
GUPTA CLOTHOUS
GUPTA FURNISHINGS
GUPTA MALL
GUPPY X PORT
WE SEND PARANDI TO THE T'ANGS
GUPTA GROCERS
VEGGIES

320-500 AD was the Golden Age of the Guptas, one of the most important imperial dynasties under which enlightened kings blossomed arts, religion and a classical culture...and entrepreneurship which led merchants and monks hurtling down the highways of Asia.

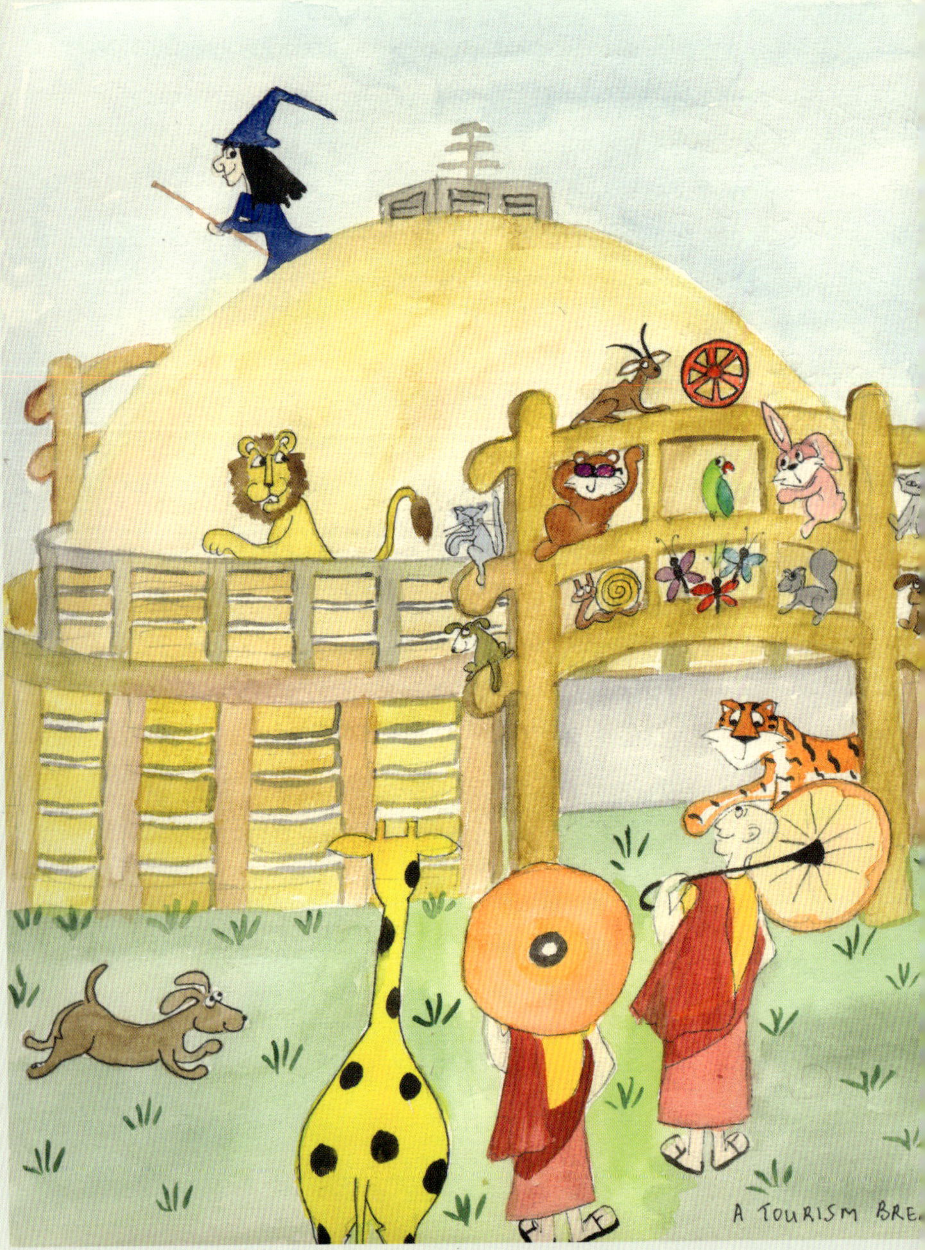
A TOURISM BRE

Lets pause for a tourism break to admire the Ruin. Sanchi was built during the reign of Ashoka. It is now a UNESCO World Heritage site.

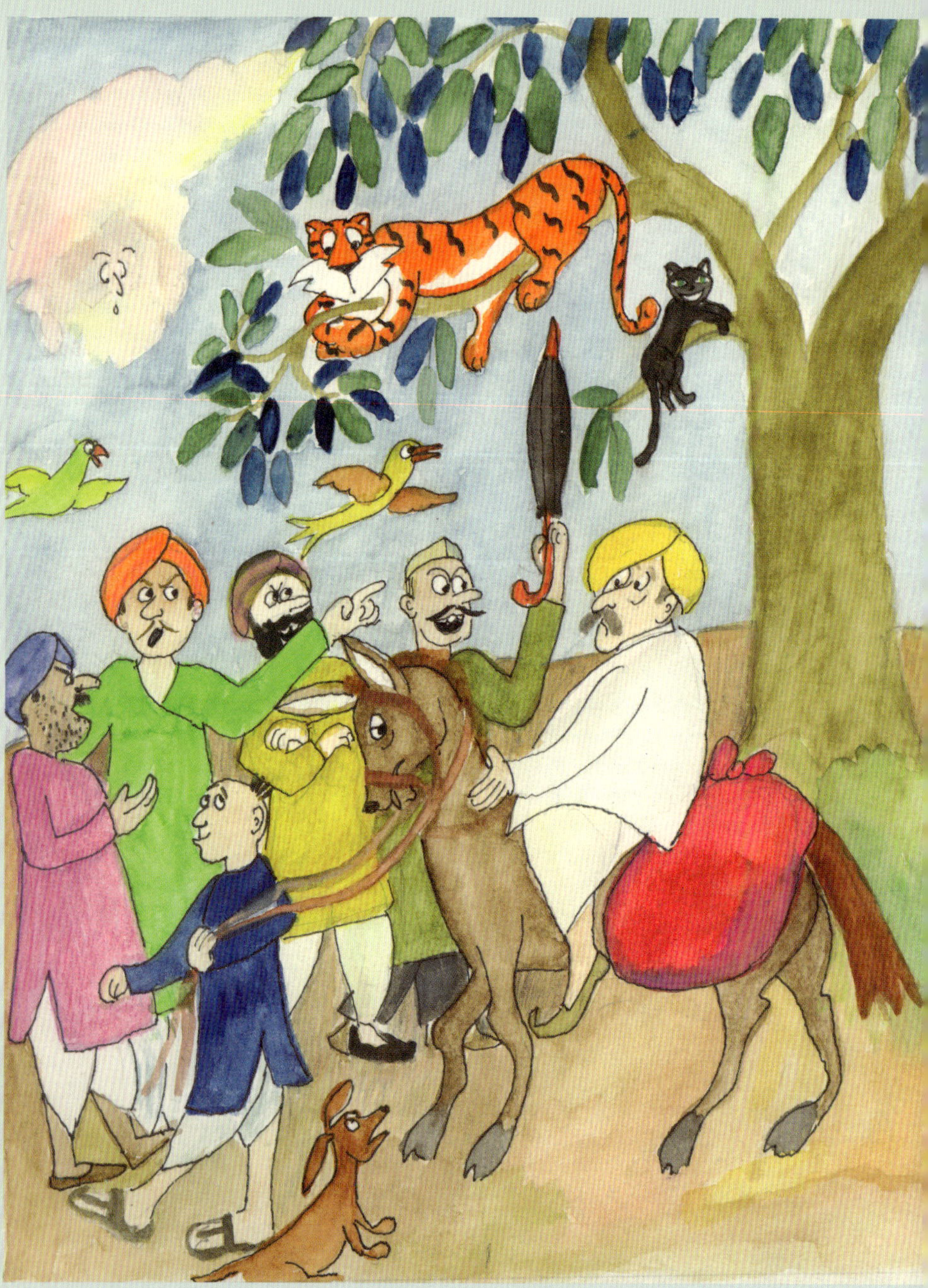

570 AD: The tales of *Panchatantra* spread to Iran. This collection of witty fables became one of the most cosmopolitan texts and entered world literature as *Kalila wa Dimna*, *Tales of Bidpai* and the *Aesop Fables*.

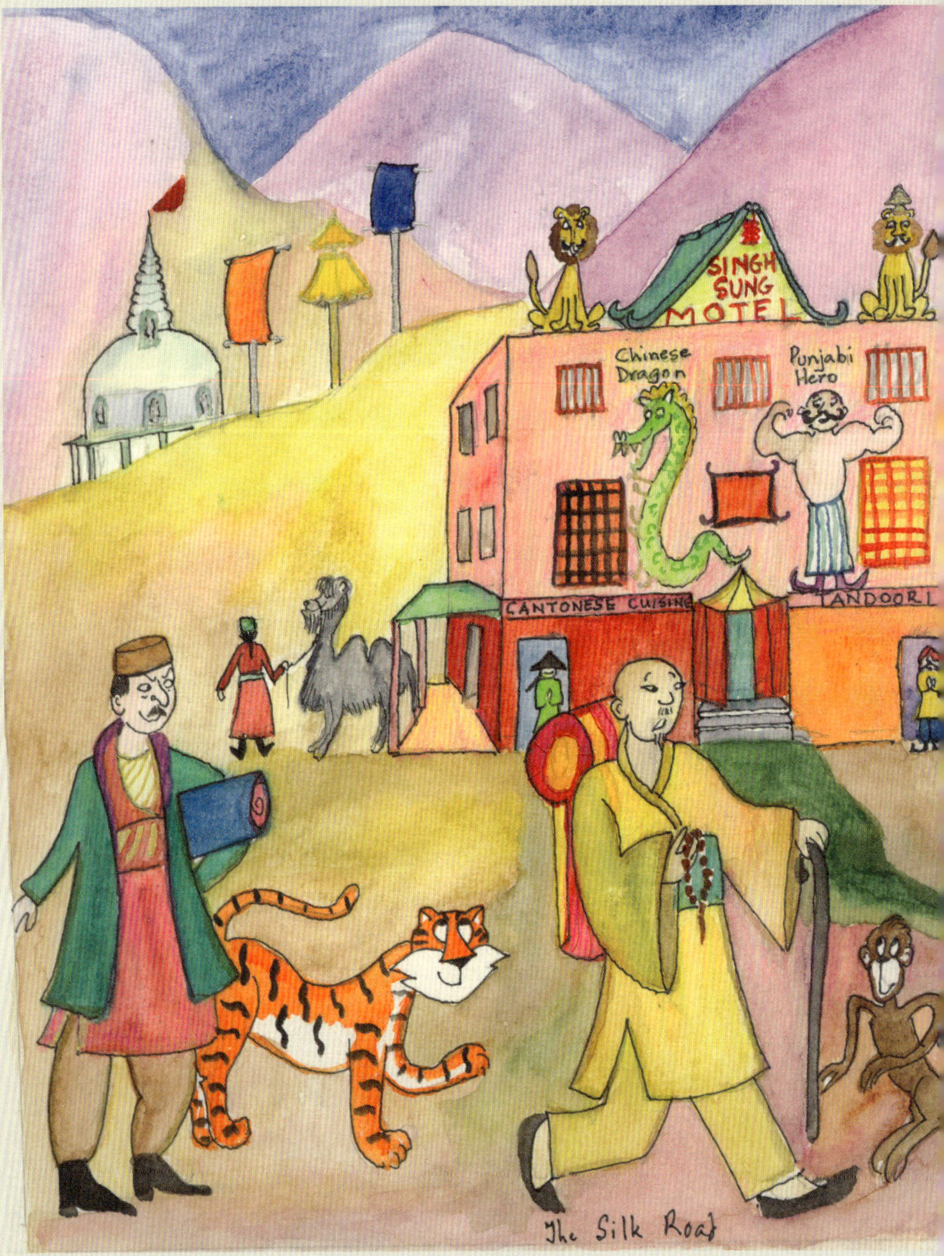
SINGH
SUNG
MOTEL
Chinese Dragon
Punjabi Hero
CANTONESE CUISINE
TANDOORI
The Silk Road

The Dharma Bums of the 6th century AD: Chinese travellers along the Silk Road, looking for nirvana and enlightenment.

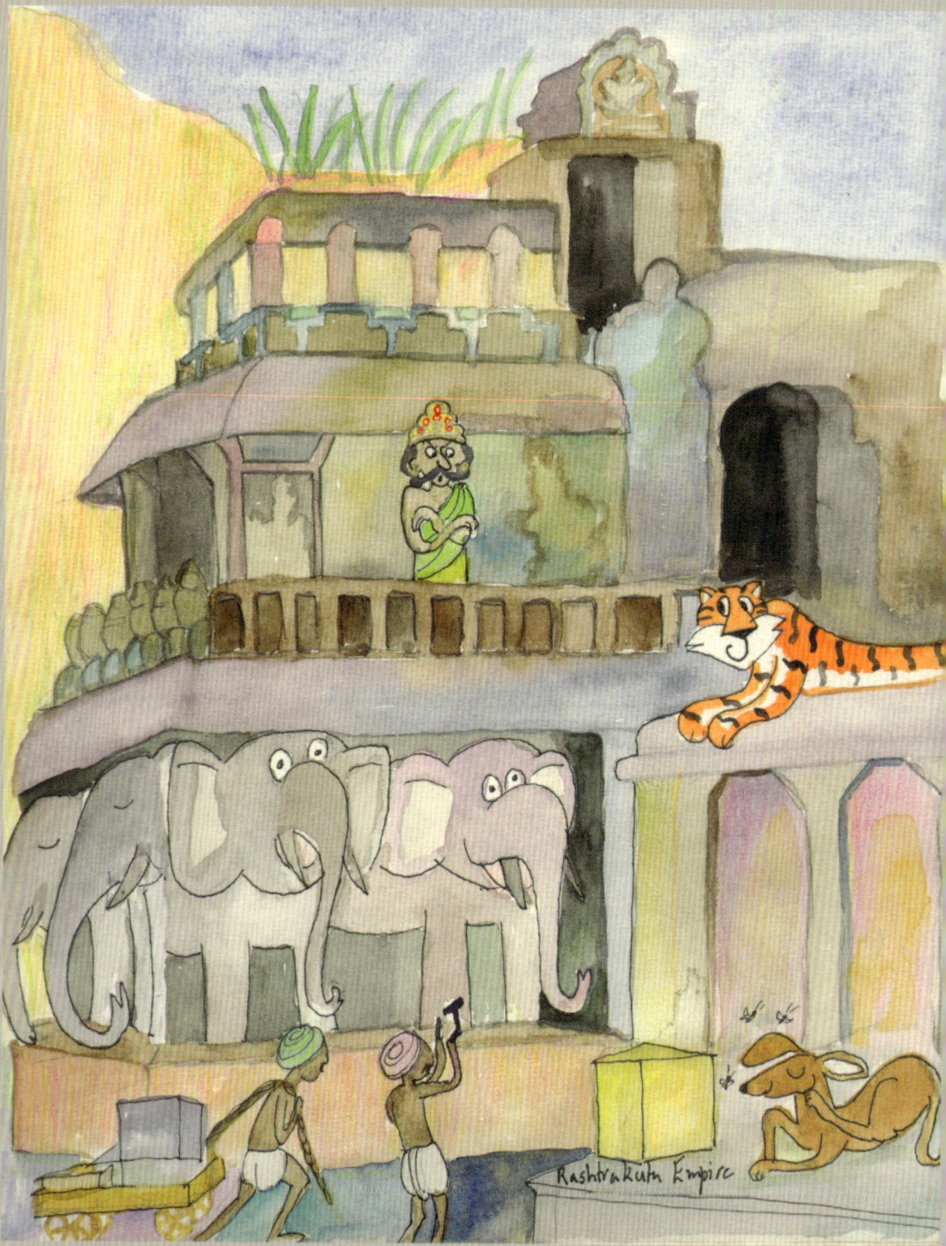
Rashtrakuta Empire

The Deccan in 790 AD: Great strides in architecture were made and the first rock cut temple was excavated at Ellora, under the Rashtrakuta kings (753-982 AD).

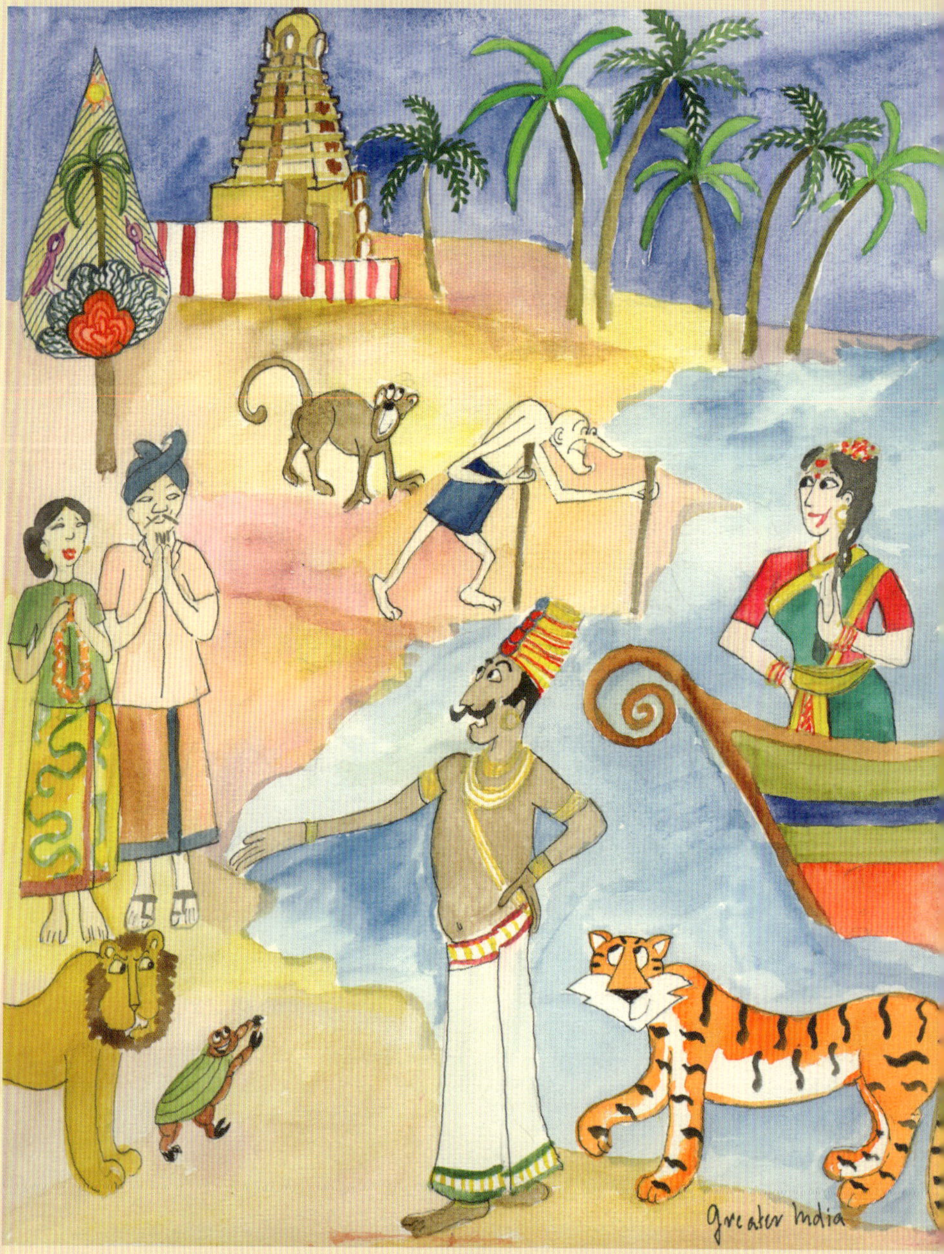
Greater India

South India: Indian civilisation and Bharatanatyam spreads to Southeast Asia under the Tamil king, Rajaraja Chola (985-1014 AD). Even today, there are flourishing Bharatanatyam dance schools in Singapore and Malaysia.

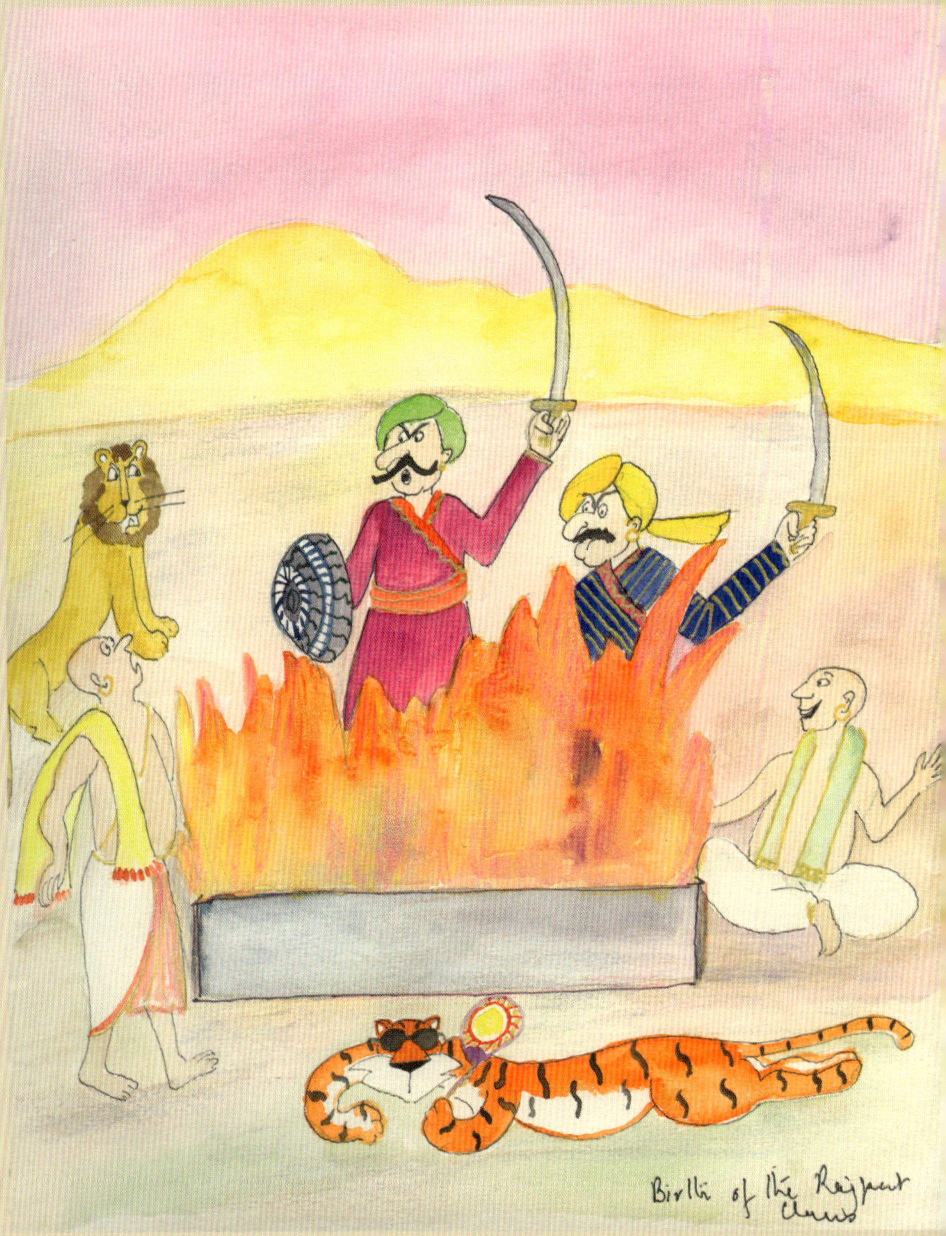
Birth of the Rajput
Clans

The Rajputs were said to have been born from the sacrificial fires of Mount Abu to protect India from foreign invaders and in the 11th century, powerful Rajput kingdoms emerged in North India and knights galloped all over the country.

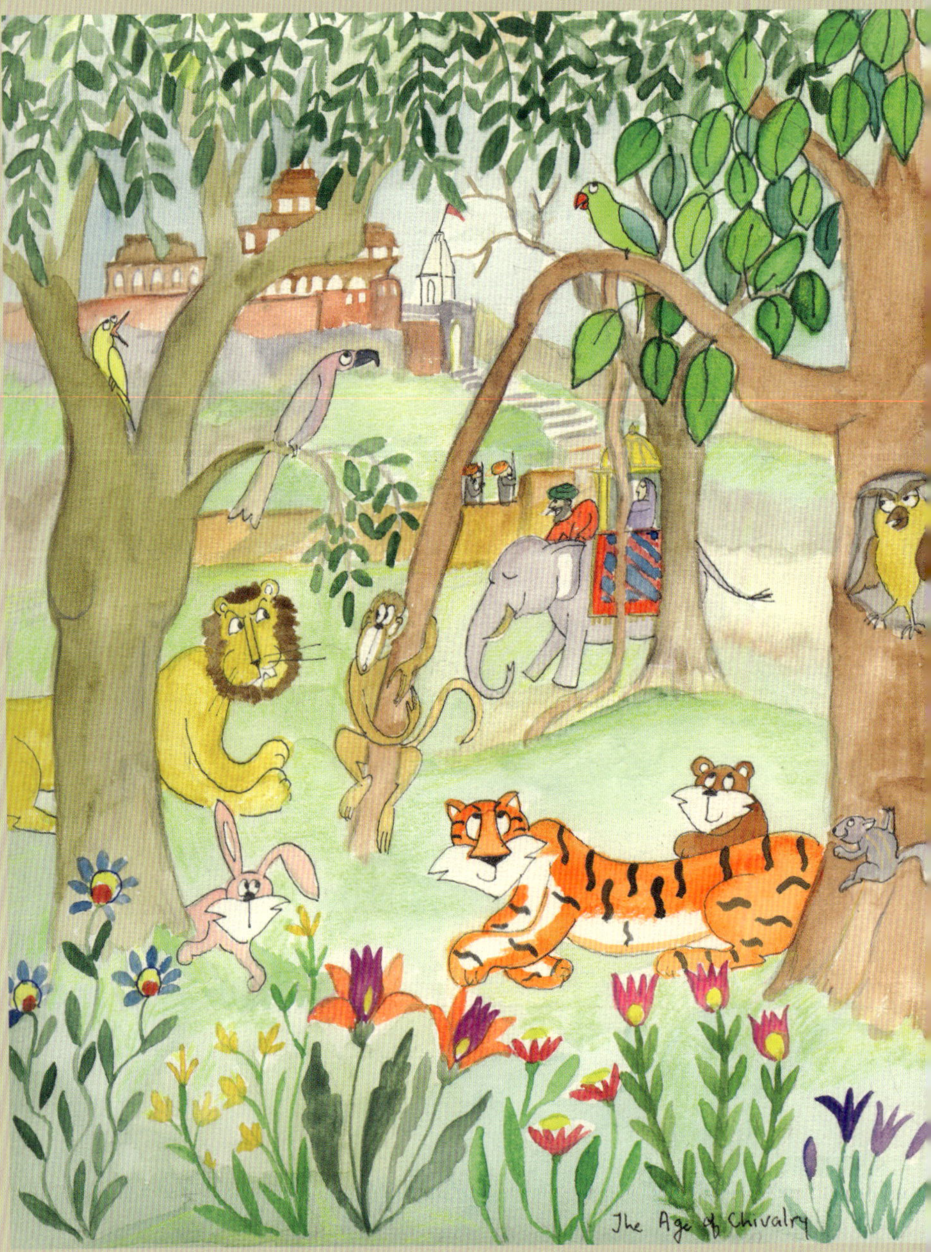
The Age of Chivalry

Theirs was the age of chivalry, when forts were built high up in inaccessible places, when brave warriors went into suicidal battles, while their women immolated themselves and bards commemorated such heroism in ballads. Now only Bollywood is Rajput...

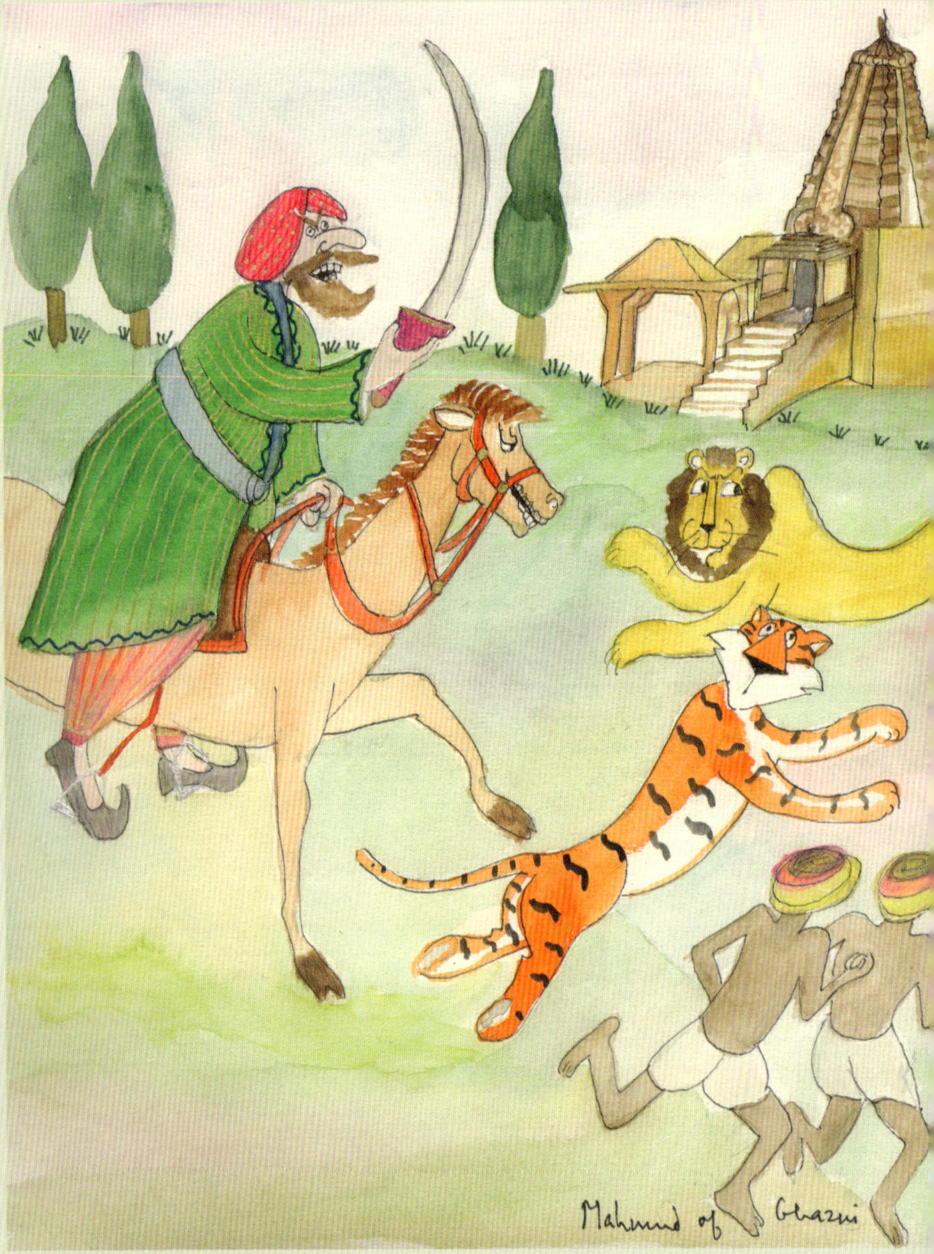
Mahmud of Ghazni

1000 AD: The terrible king, Mahmud of Ghazni (present-day Afghanistan) made repeated raids in India and looted the rich Gujarati temple of Somnath. Imagine how much wealth there was that he had to repeatedly raid it!

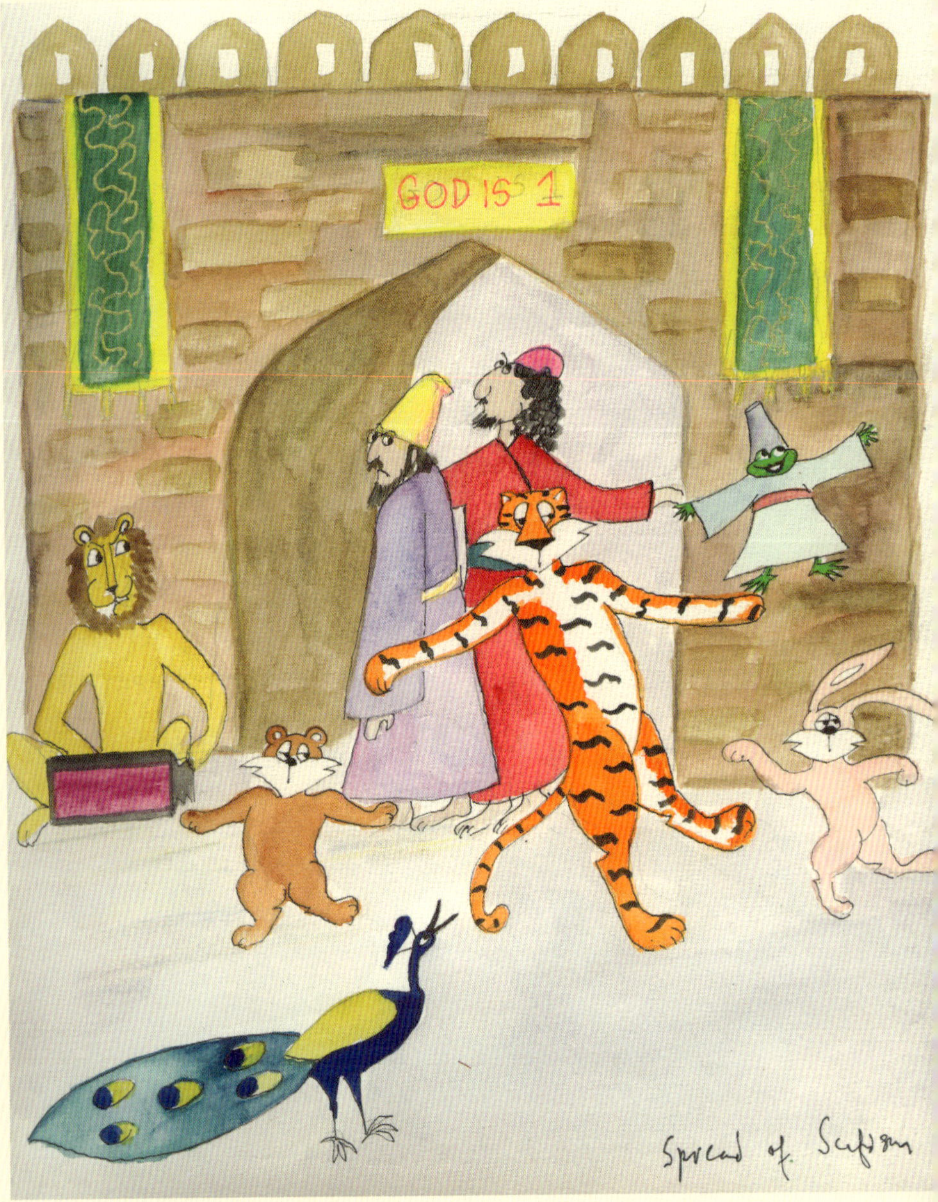

With the first Muslim conquests at the end of the 12th century, came the Sufis. Thus, the Whirling Dervishes of Sufism whirled and twirled all over India, establishing their centres or *khanqahs*.

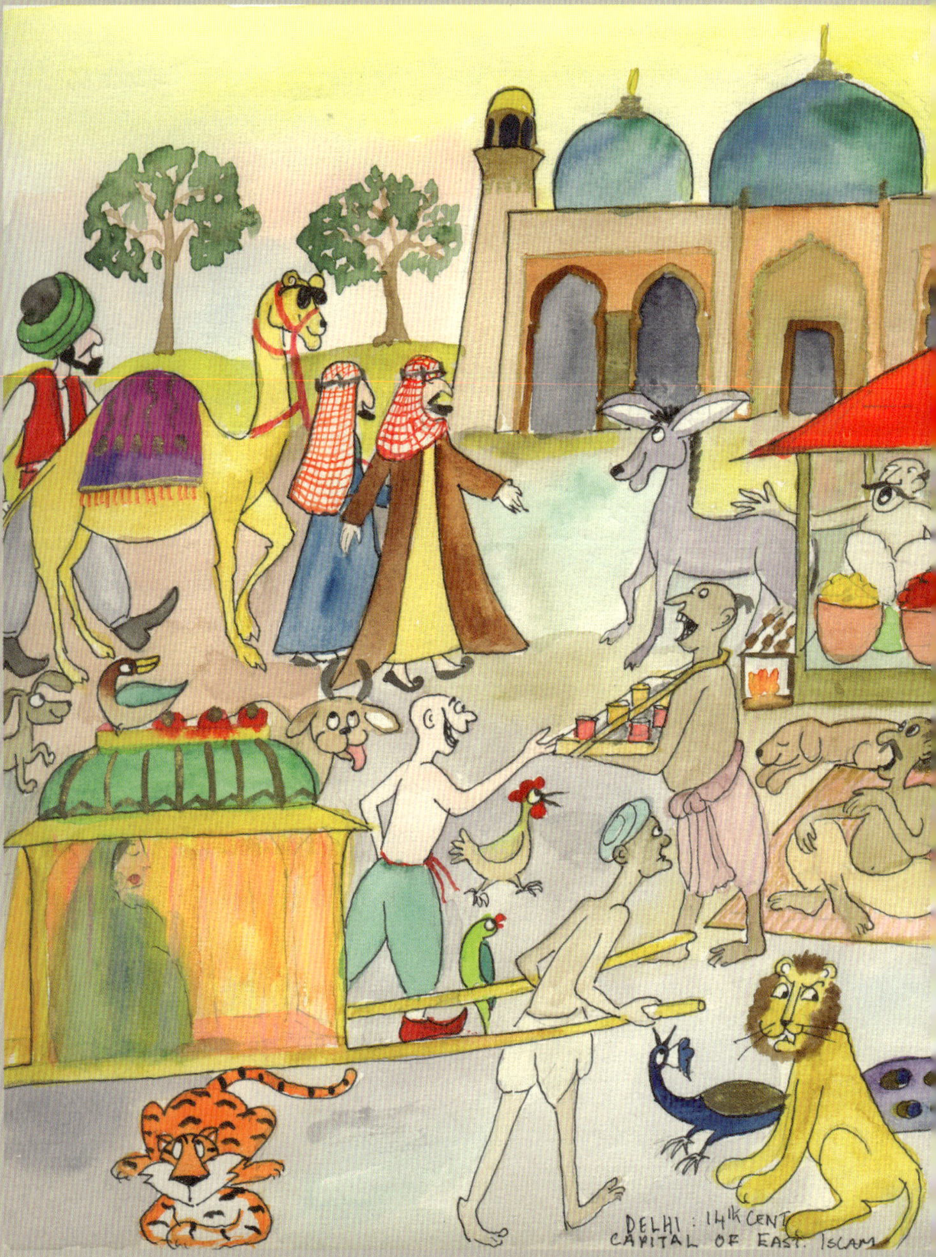
DELHI : 14th CENT
CAPITAL OF EAST. ISLAM

By the 14th century, the great cities of Asia were destroyed by the Mongol hordes of Genghiz Khan and his ilk, but Delhi survived and became the centrepiece of Islamic intellectual and cultural life as all the great scholars of Islam took refuge with the Sultanate.

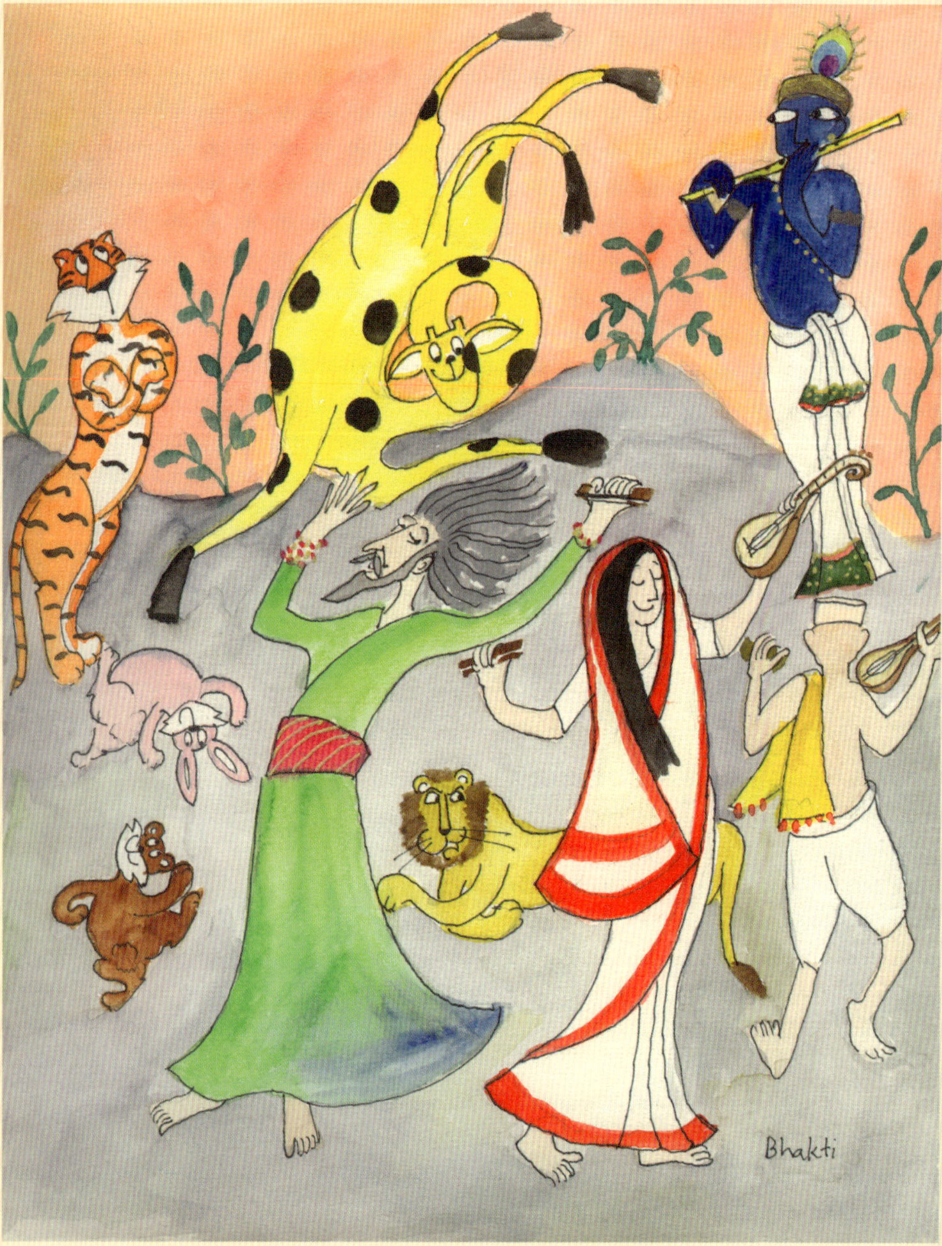
Bhakti

In the 14th century, mystics and saints wandered throughout the country spreading the message of *bhakti* or devotion to God, which went beyond the orthodoxy of caste and ritual. This was the ancestor of the Hare Krishna movement of our times.

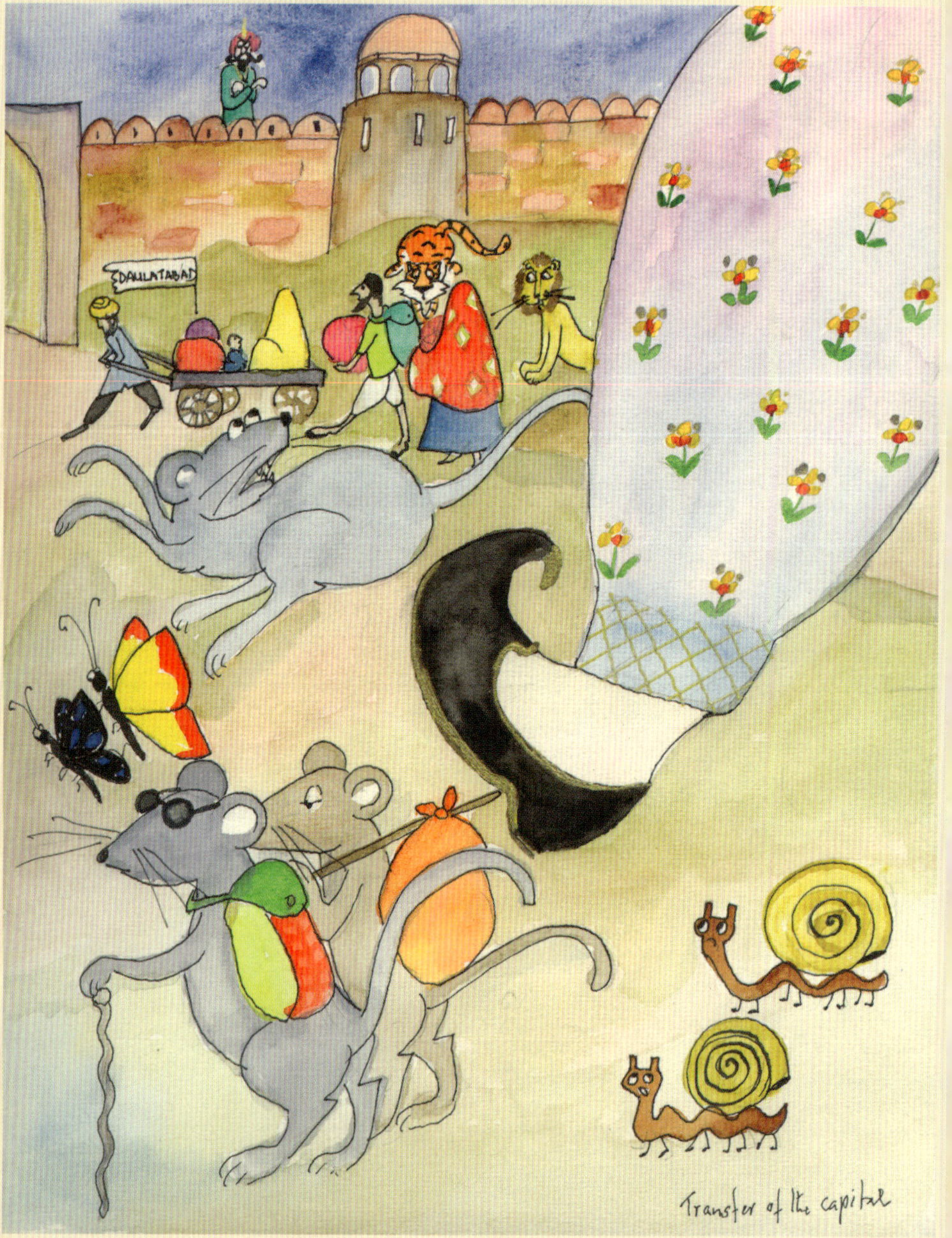
DAULATABAD
Transfer of the capital

From 1325-1351, Mohammed bin Tughluq was the Sultan of Delhi. As his empire grew and as the Mongols galloped around Central Asia, he felt that a capital 1,500 kms south of Delhi was necessary, so he kicked every creature in the city southwards.

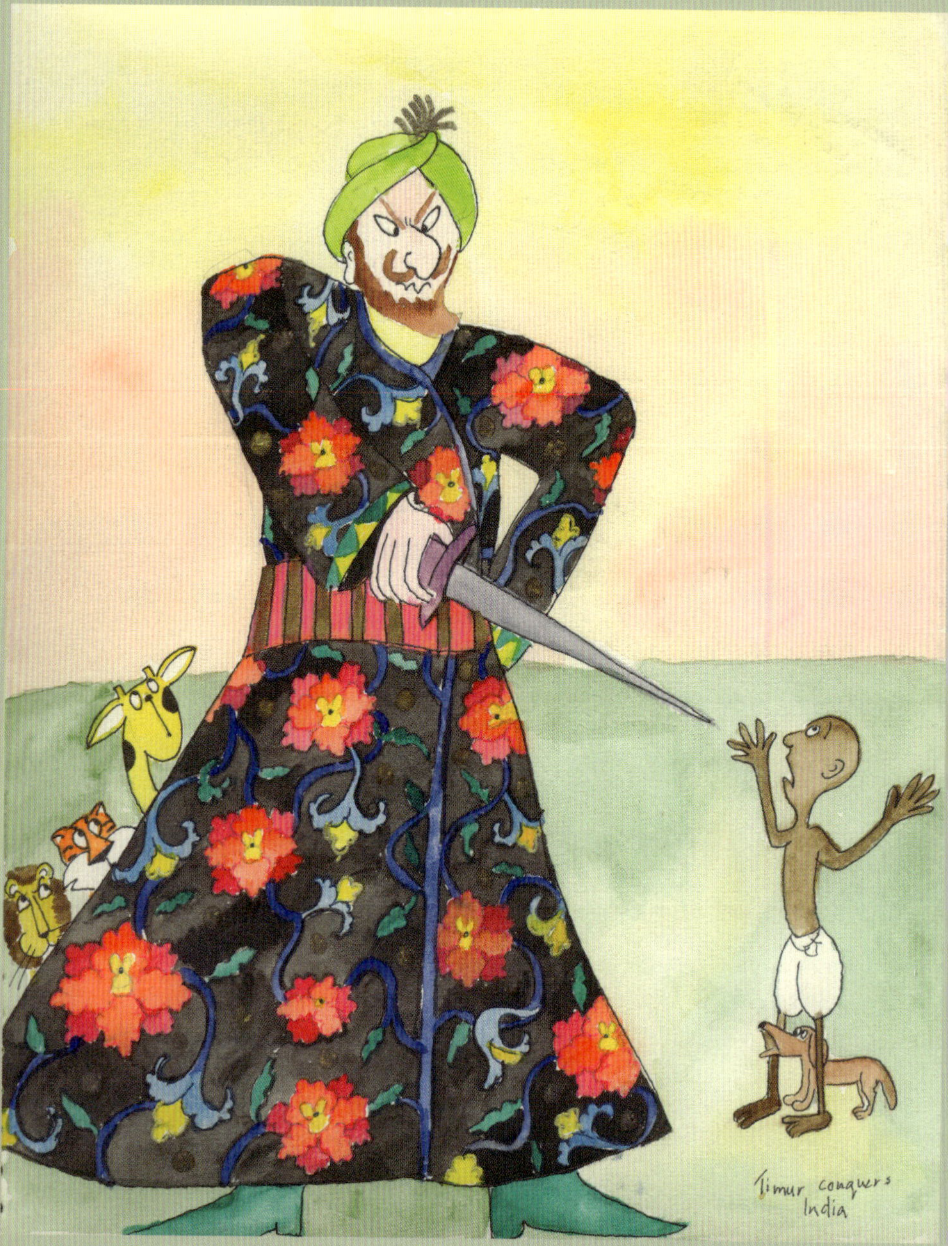
Timur conquers India

1398: The dreaded King of Samarkand, Timur the Lame, conquered India and devastated Delhi. Do you know he carried away all our craftsmen to beautify Samarkand, which as you know is very beautiful. Have you taken the Golden Road to it?

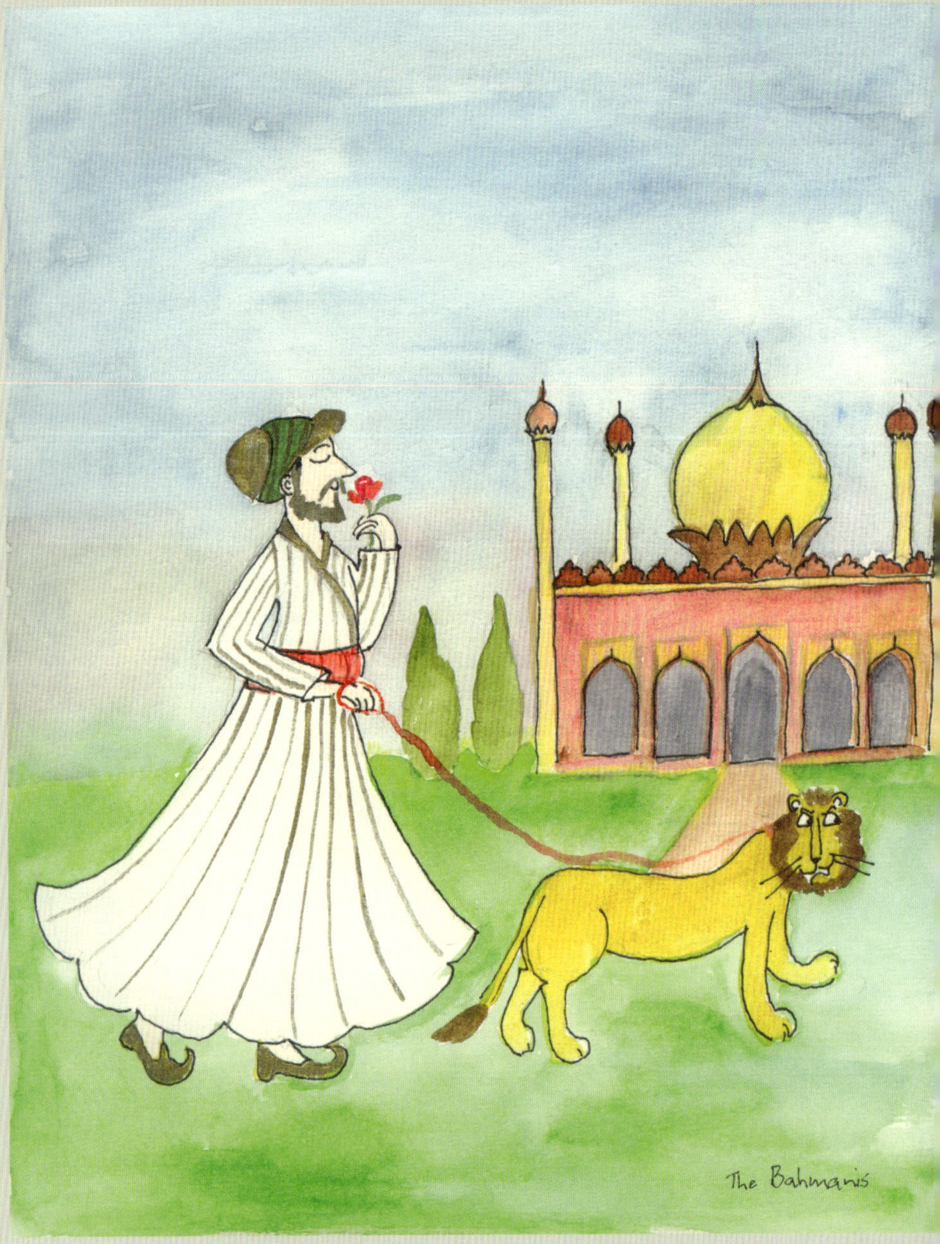
The Bahmanis

Alauddin Hassan Bahman Shah, cool guy, revolted against his boss, Mohammed bin Tughluq in 1347. He founded the Bahamani Sultanate, the first Muslim state in the Deccan and with the patronage of these Deccani Sultans, some of the best biryanis were invented.

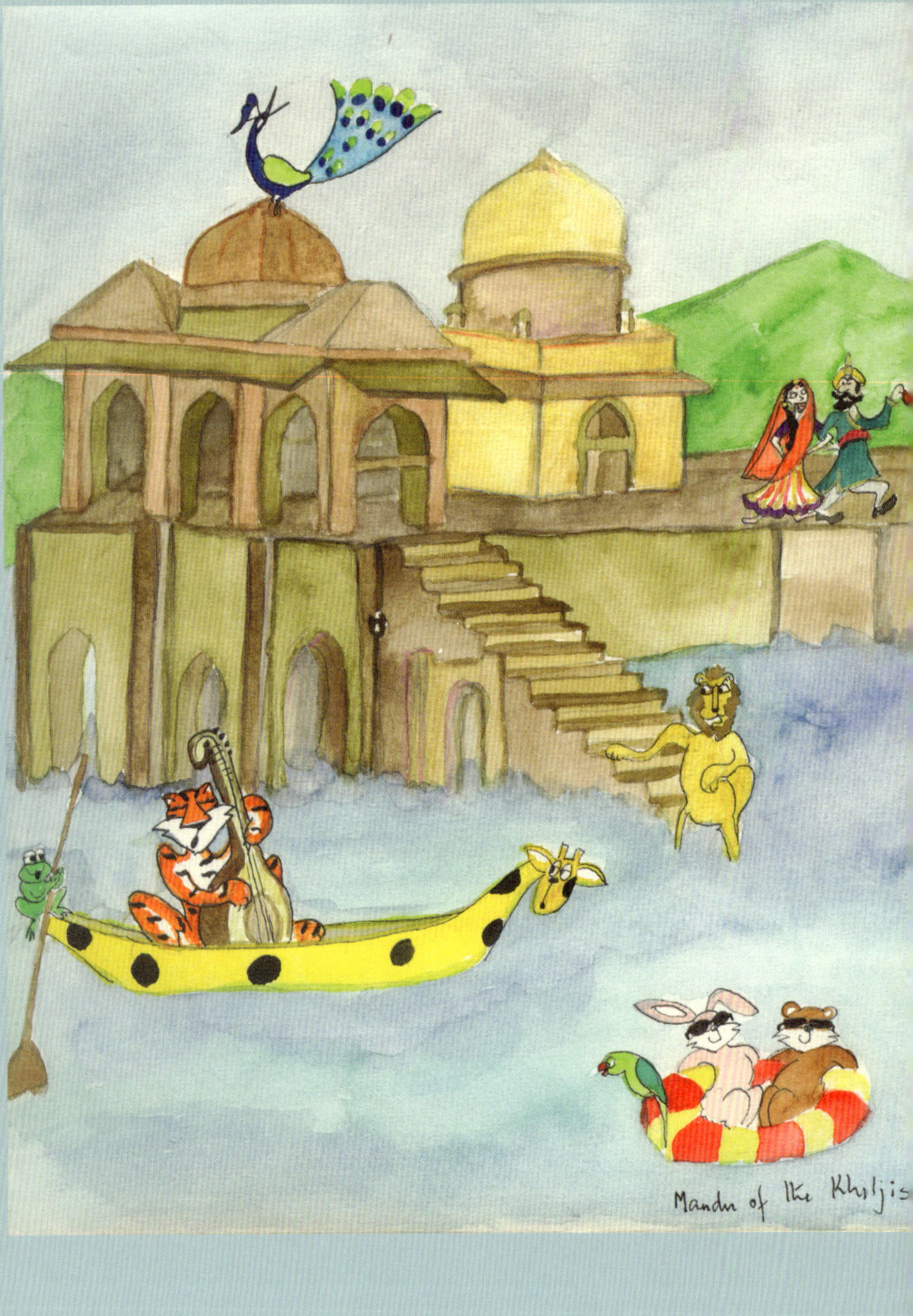
Mandu of the Khiljis

1392: Mandu was founded in Central India on the shattered remains of the Tughluq Sultanate. Famous for its architecture, painting, music and a cookery book. Visit it during the monsoons and experience the magic of its ruins...

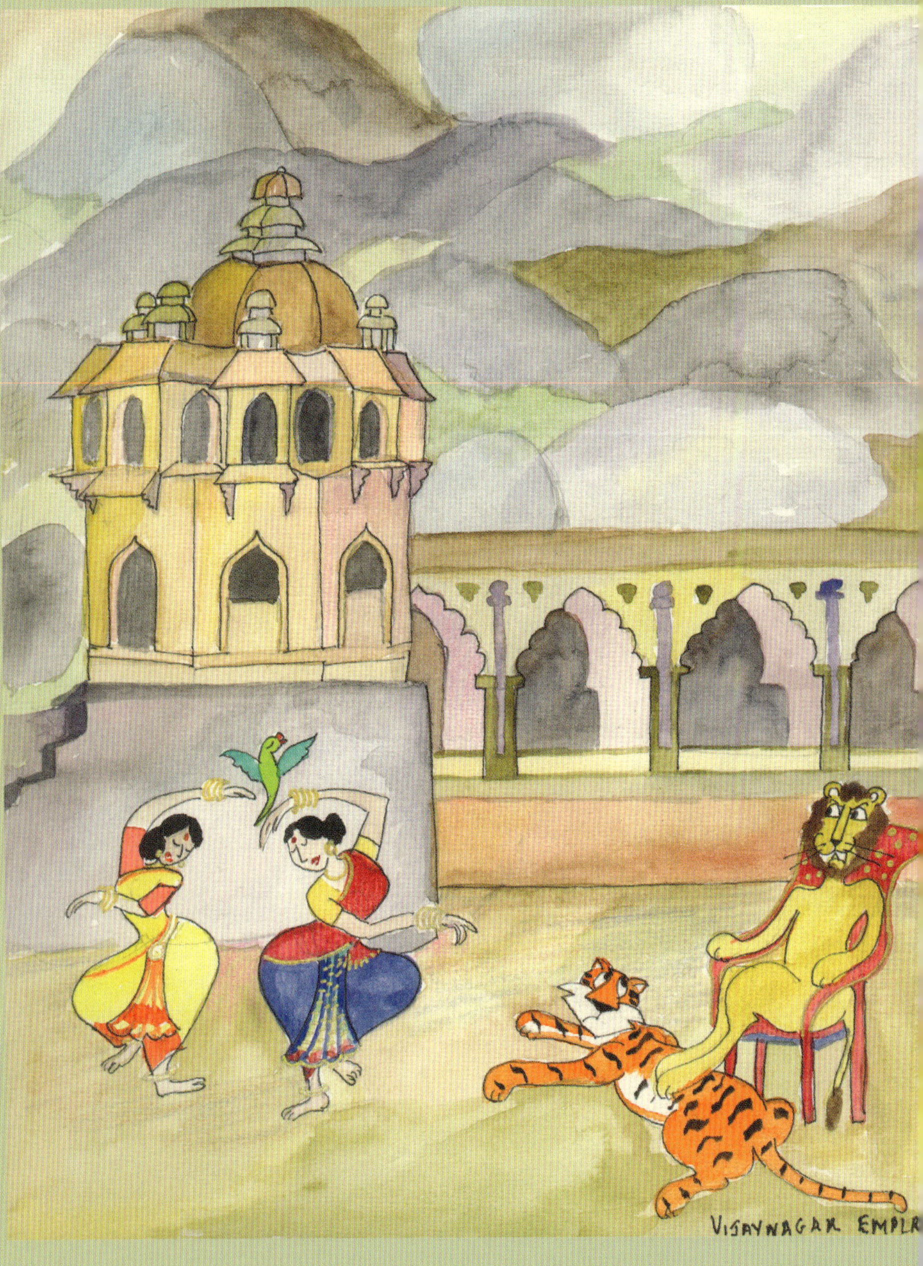
VIJAYNAGAR EMPIR

The last great Hindu kingdom of Vijaynagar flourished at the end of the 15th century. So great was its wealth that rubies, emeralds and pearls were sold on the streets of Hampi, its capital city. Truly it was a "Wow" kingdom.

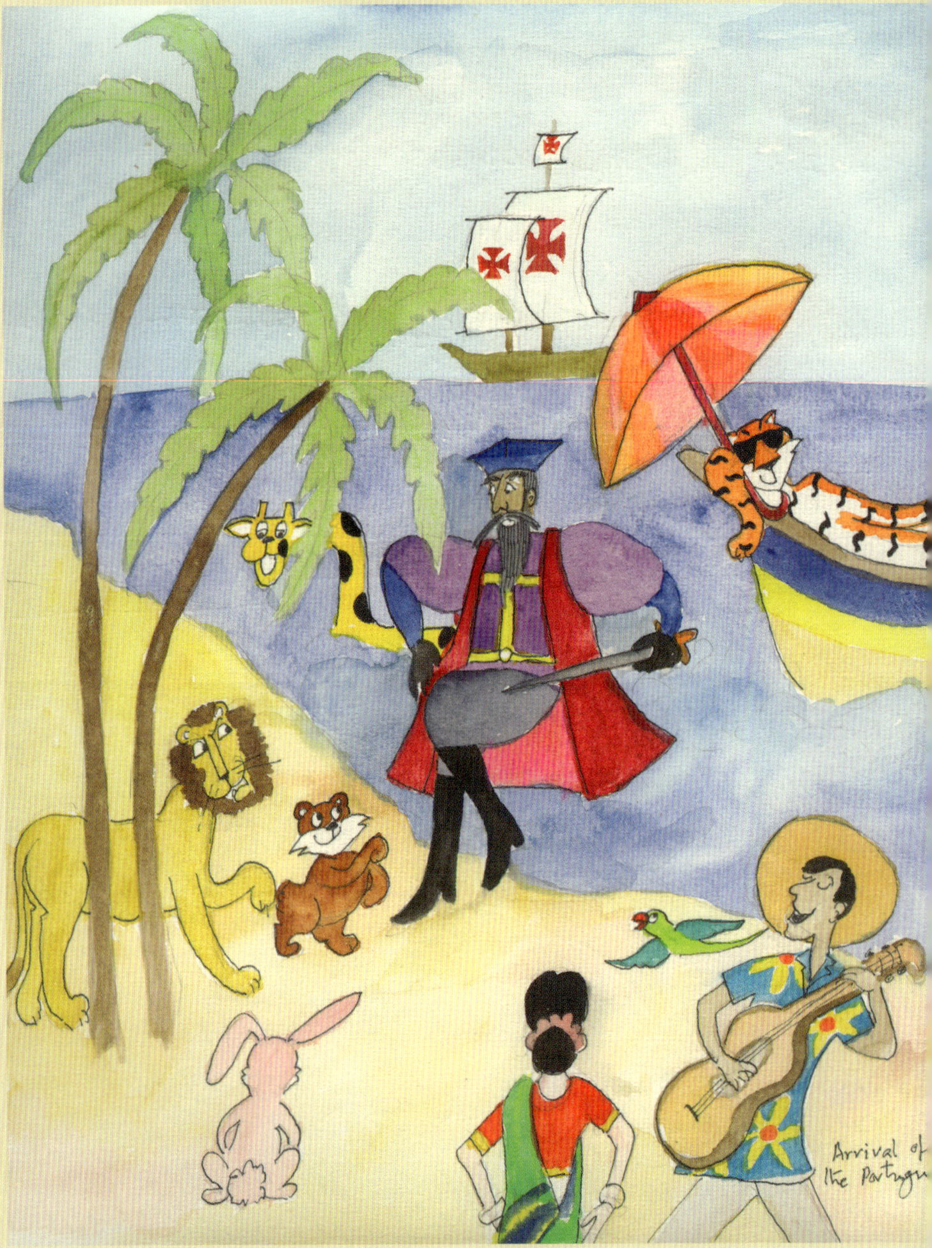
Arrival of
the

In 1498, Vasco da Gama discovered the sea route to India and in 1510, the Portuguese conquered Goa with sword, cross and fado. They were met by locals singing the *mando* and all of them got together to make Goa into a great paradise for lotus eaters.

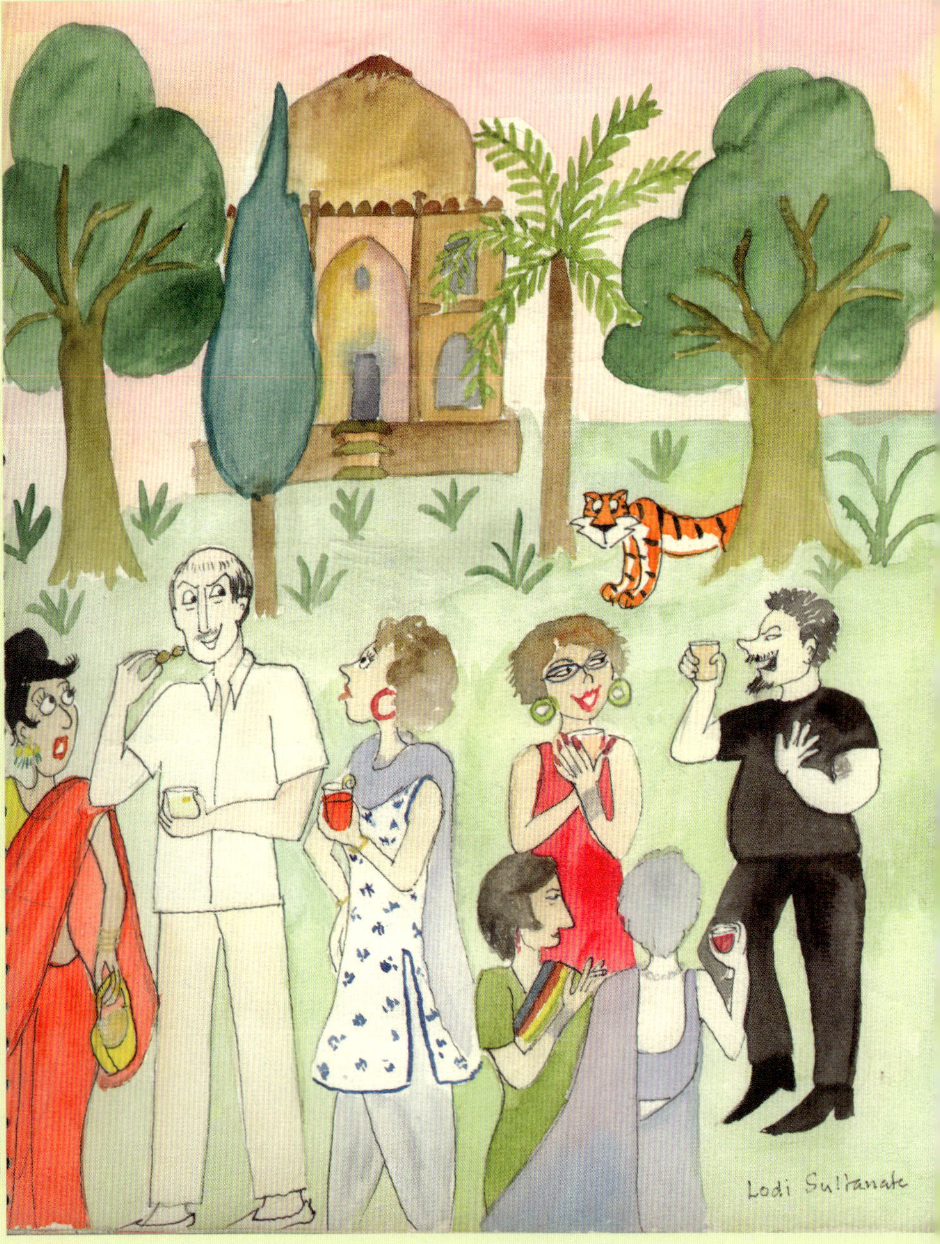
Lodi Sultanate

2010: Cocktails in Lodi Gardens, where the Lodi Sultans of Delhi rest and where we too can have a bit of “R and R”.

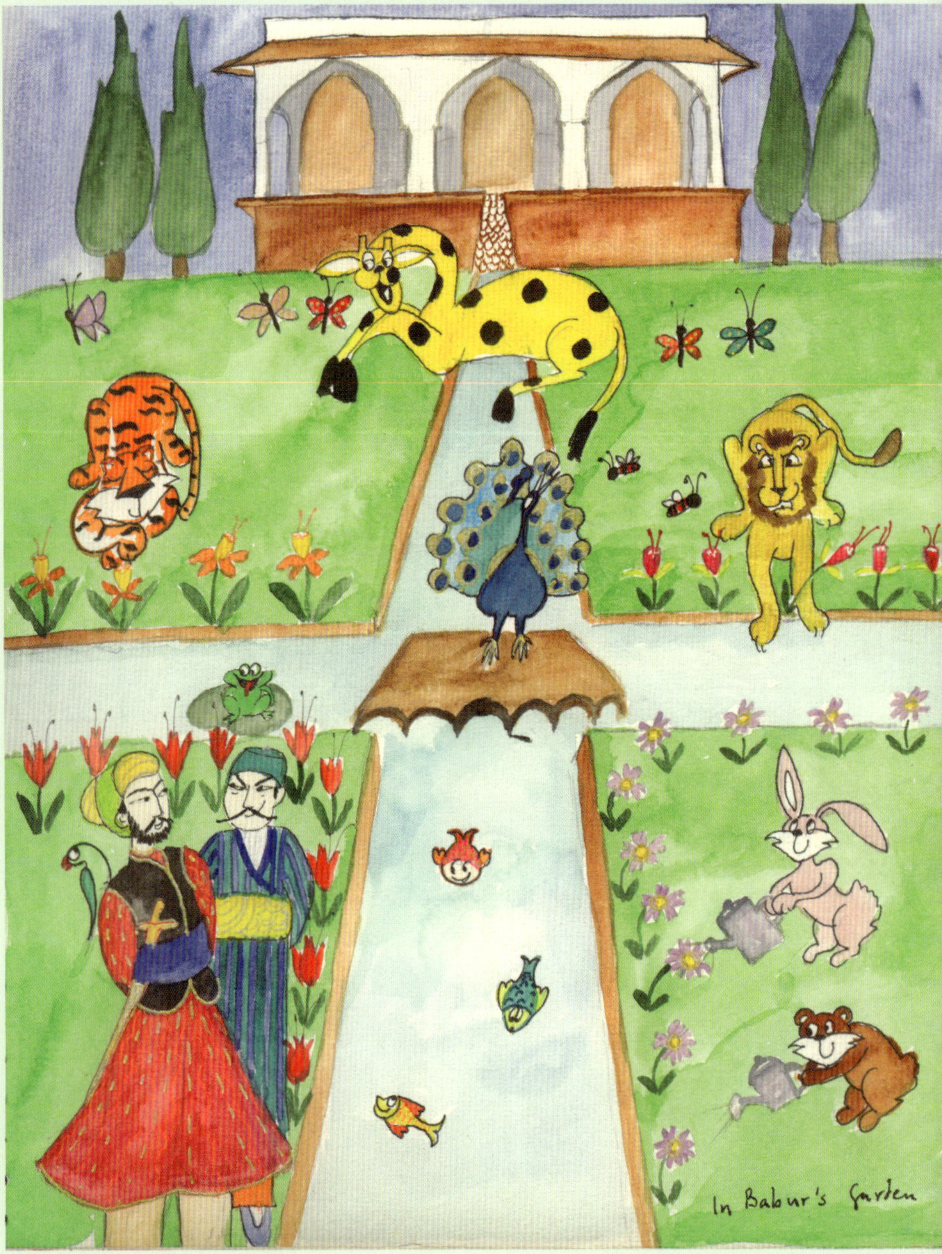
In Babur's Garden

1526: Babur, the Mughal, defeated the last Lodi Sultan with gunfire, the first time it was heard in India. He invented the Mughal garden and also the Mughal Empire.

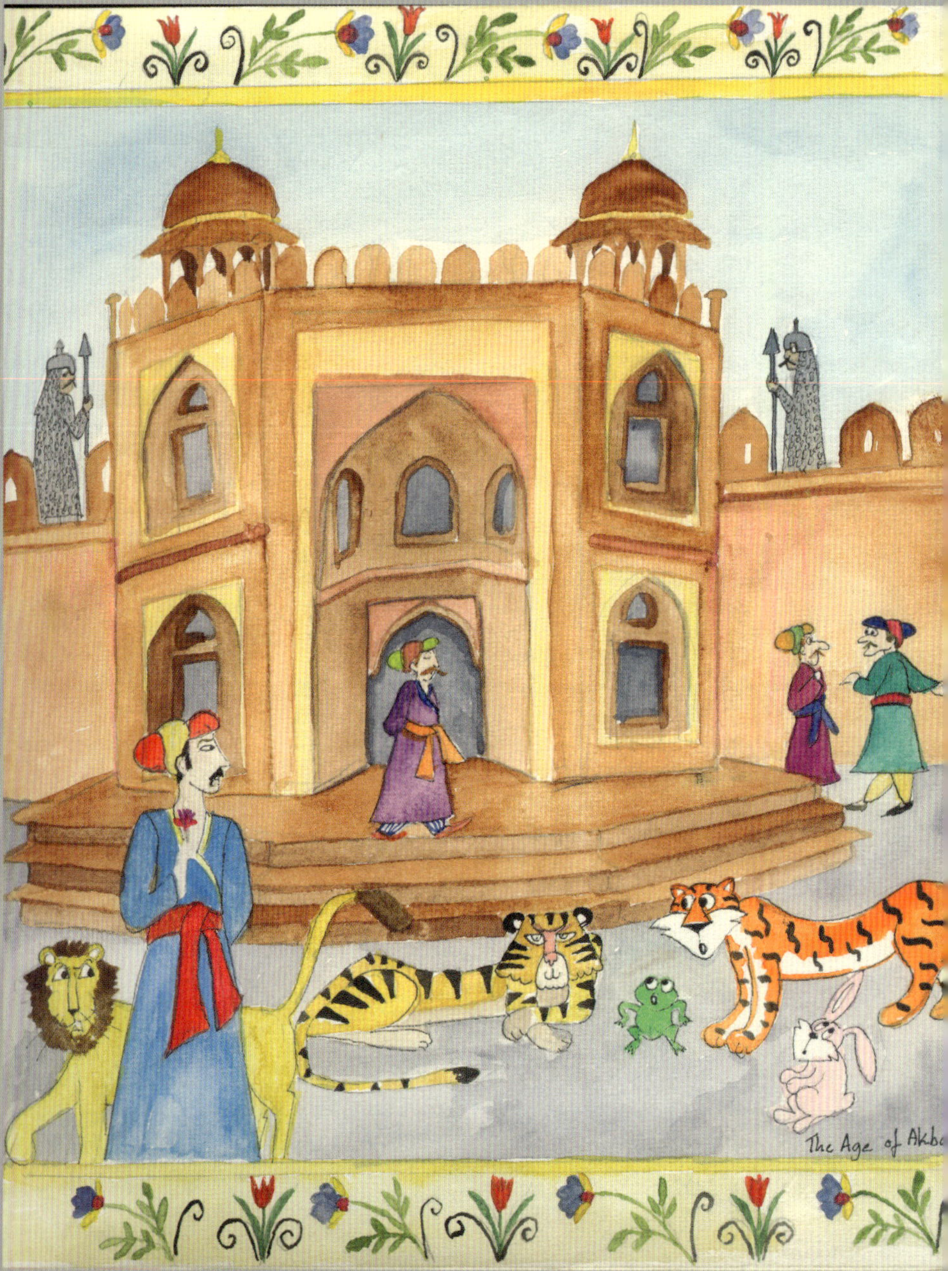
The Age of Akb

His grandson Akbar (1556-1605) was the greatest Mughal Emperor. He did many things including the founding of an eclectic religion, Din-i-Illahi; conquered forts; and built the gorgeous city of Fatehpur Sikri, which alas he soon deserted because it ran out of water.

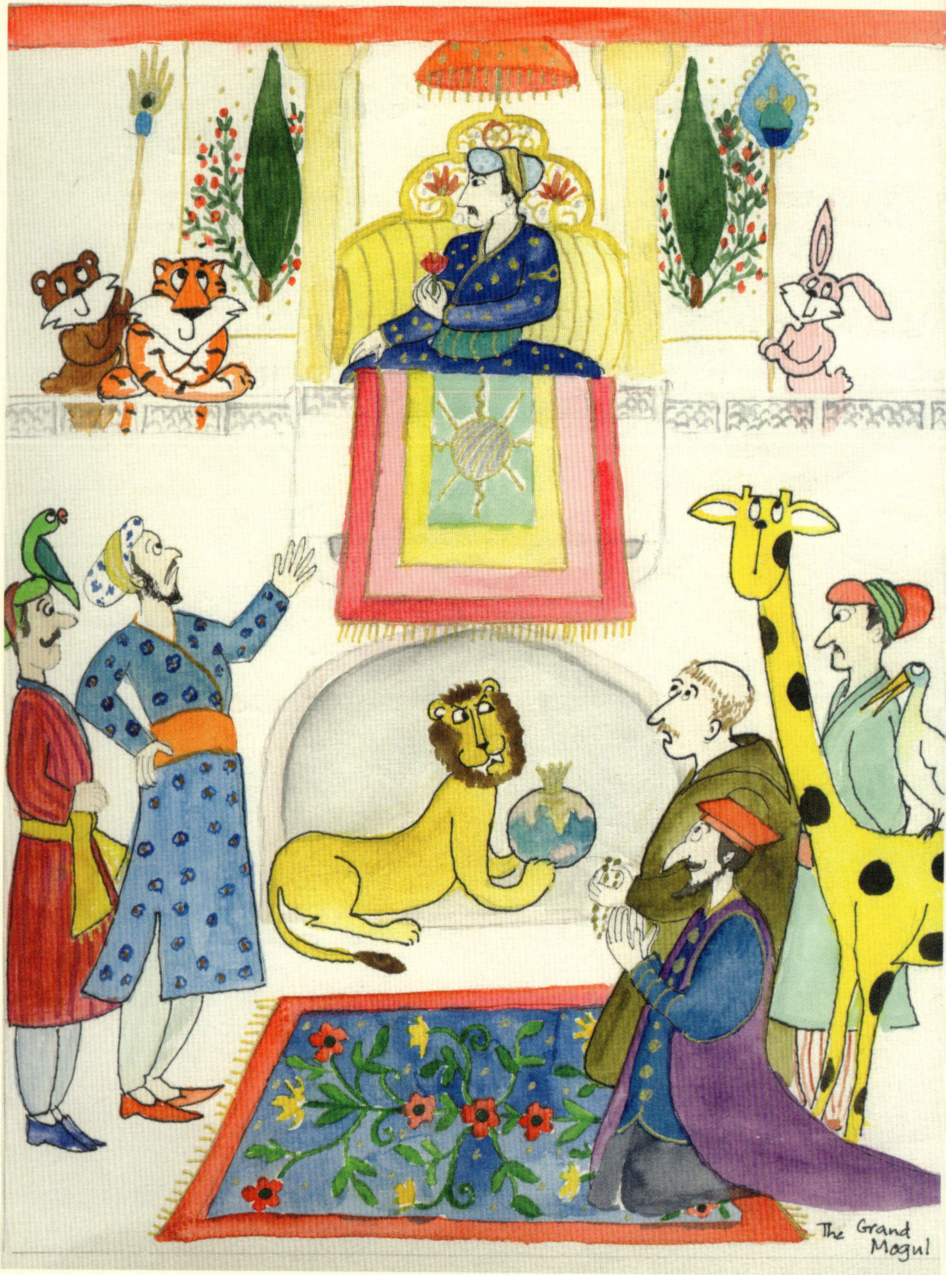
The Grand Mogul

The Grand Mughal Shah Jahan (1628-58) received several foreign ambassadors at his court in Delhi. It was his father, Jahangir, who granted trading rights to the British; note this as it had serious repercussions.

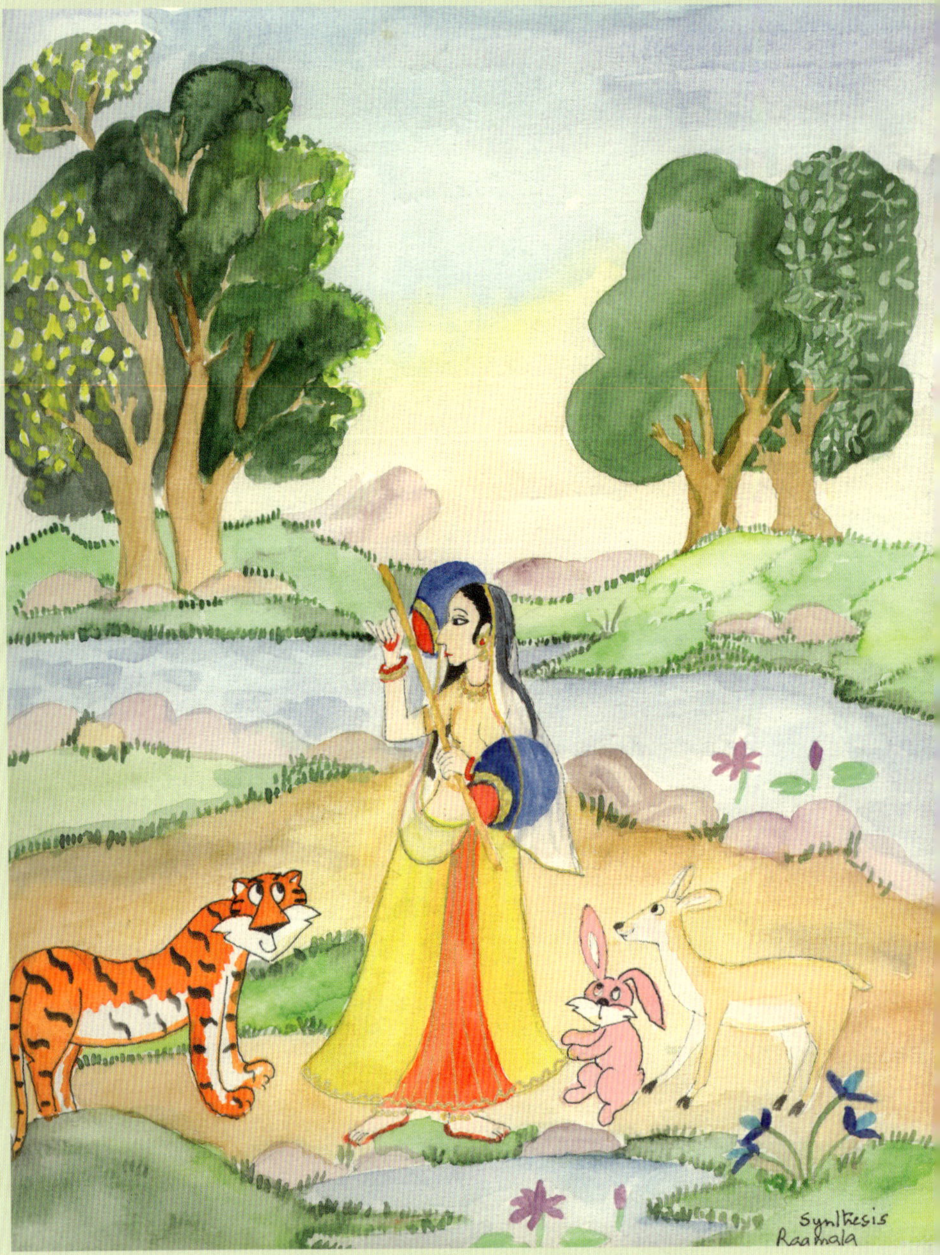
Synthesis
Raamala

In the 18th century, decline began to set in and Mughal painters sought refuge in the hill states Kangra, Guler, Basholi. A hybrid genre of painting emerged which expressed the beauties of nature in a lyrical and delicate style.

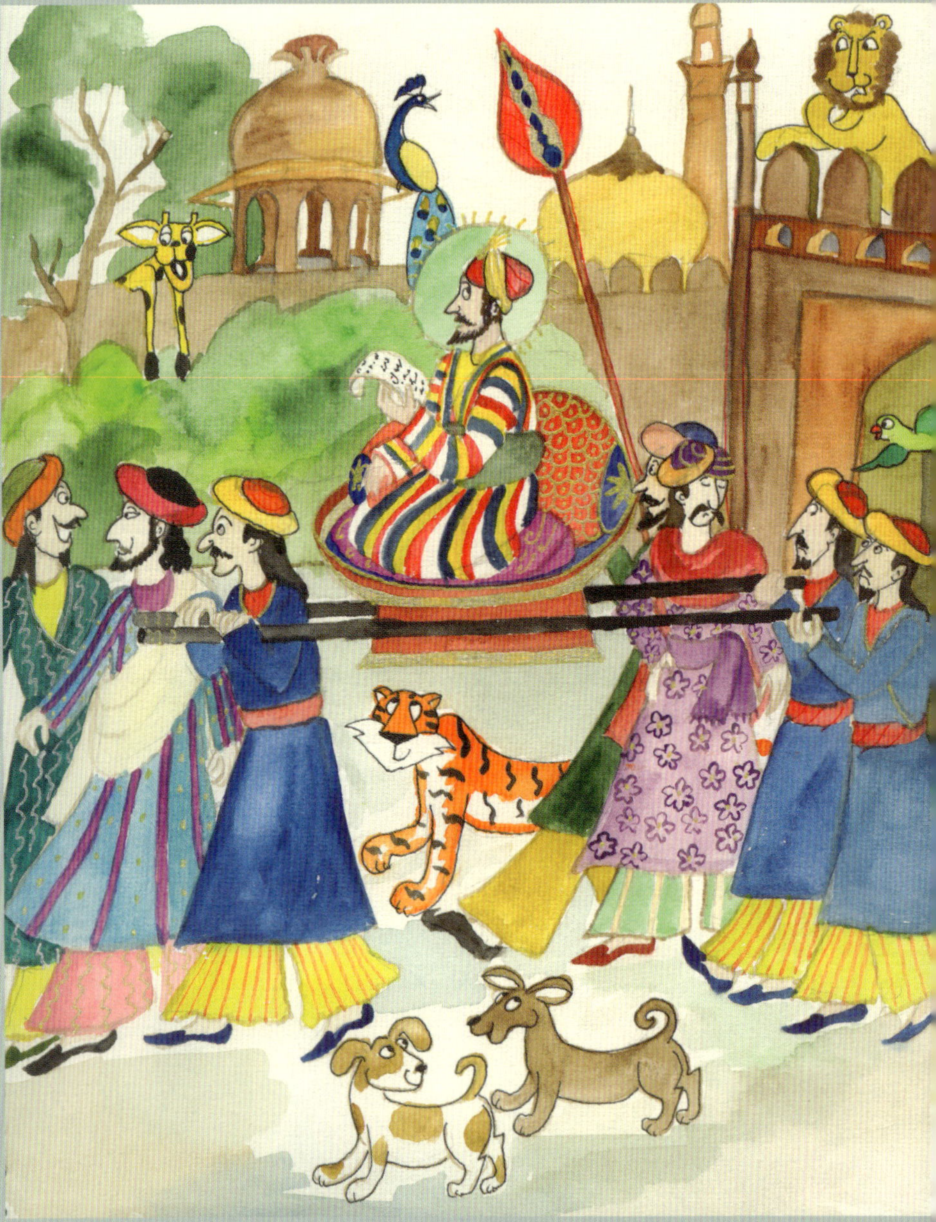

Shah Alam's empire was from Delhi to Palam (1728-1806), which is now the Indira Gandhi International airport in New Delhi. Poor Mughals, how have the mighty fallen!

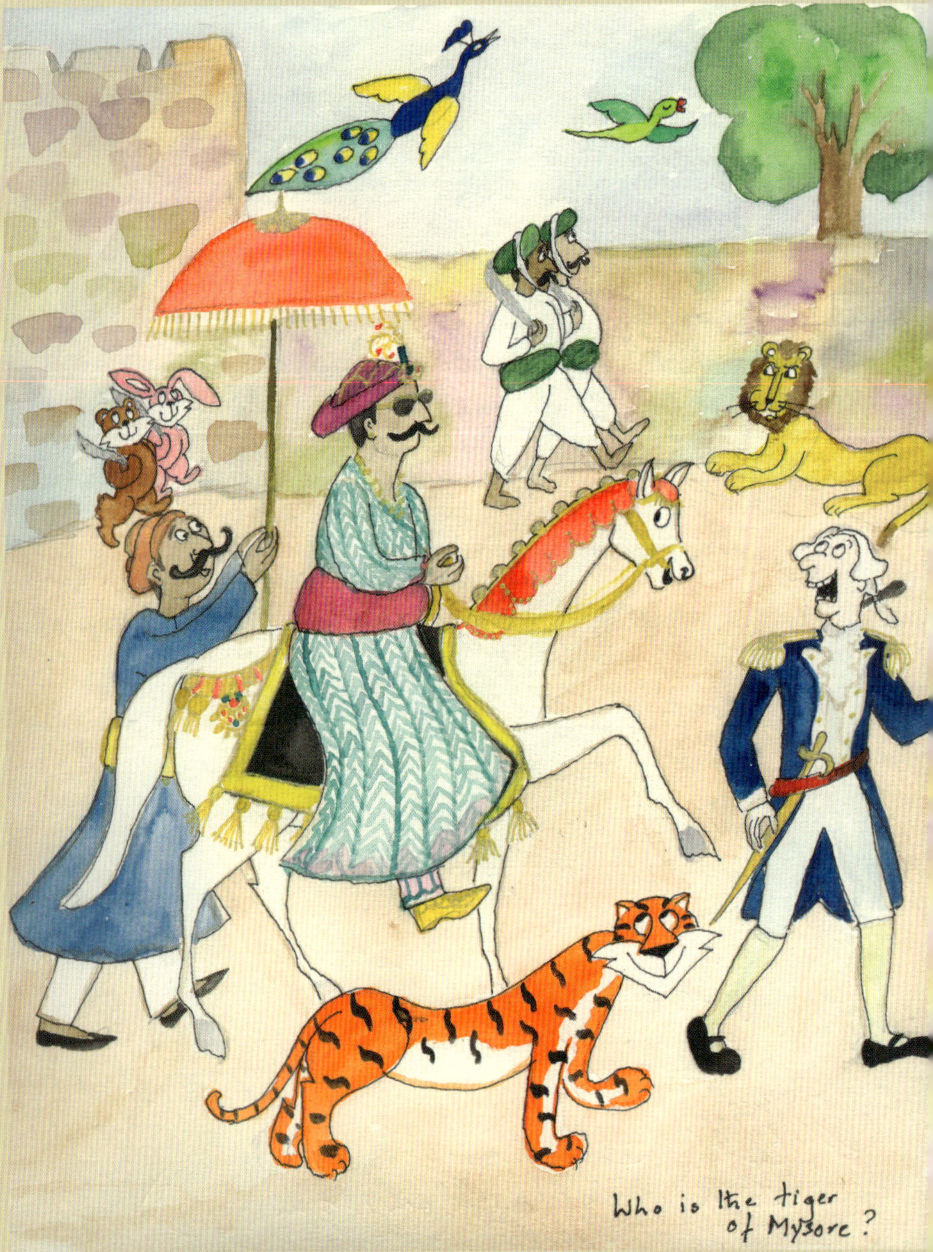
Who is the tiger of Mysore?

"Who is the Tiger of Mysore?" Tipu Sultan (1750-1799): He was King of Mysore and very friendly with the French who were settled in Pondicherry. The British did not like him and hated his letter-writing to Napoleon Bonaparte. So they went hammer and tongs and finally defeated and killed him in Srirangapatnam.

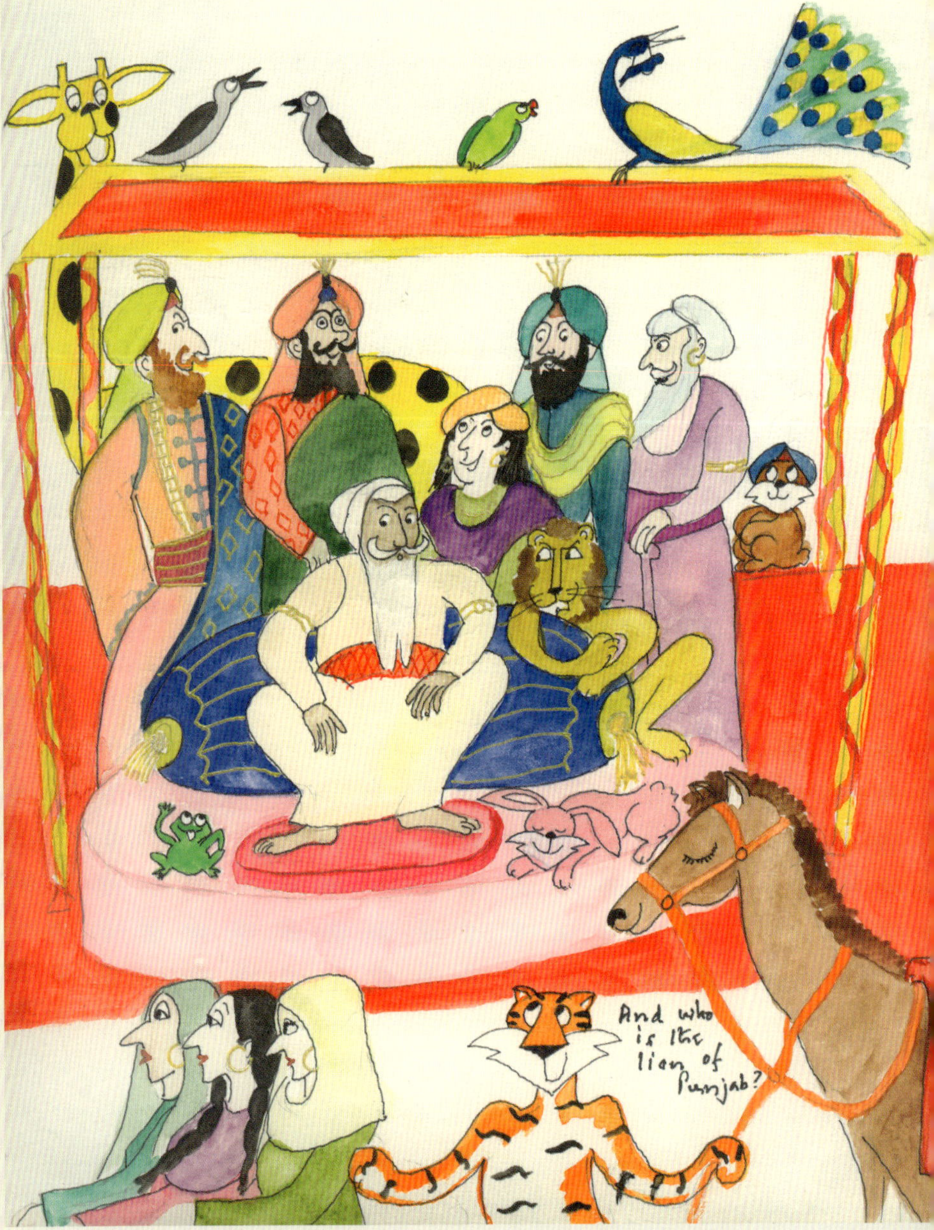
And who is the lion of Punjab?

"Who is the Lion of the Punjab?"
Ranjit Singh (1790-1839):
He founded the Sikh empire that included large tracts of Afghanistan, the borders of Tibet and huge amounts of North India and Pakistan. It was said of him: "The Maharaja is like the sun and sun has only one eye. The splendor and luminosity of his single eye is so much that I have never dared to look at his other eye."

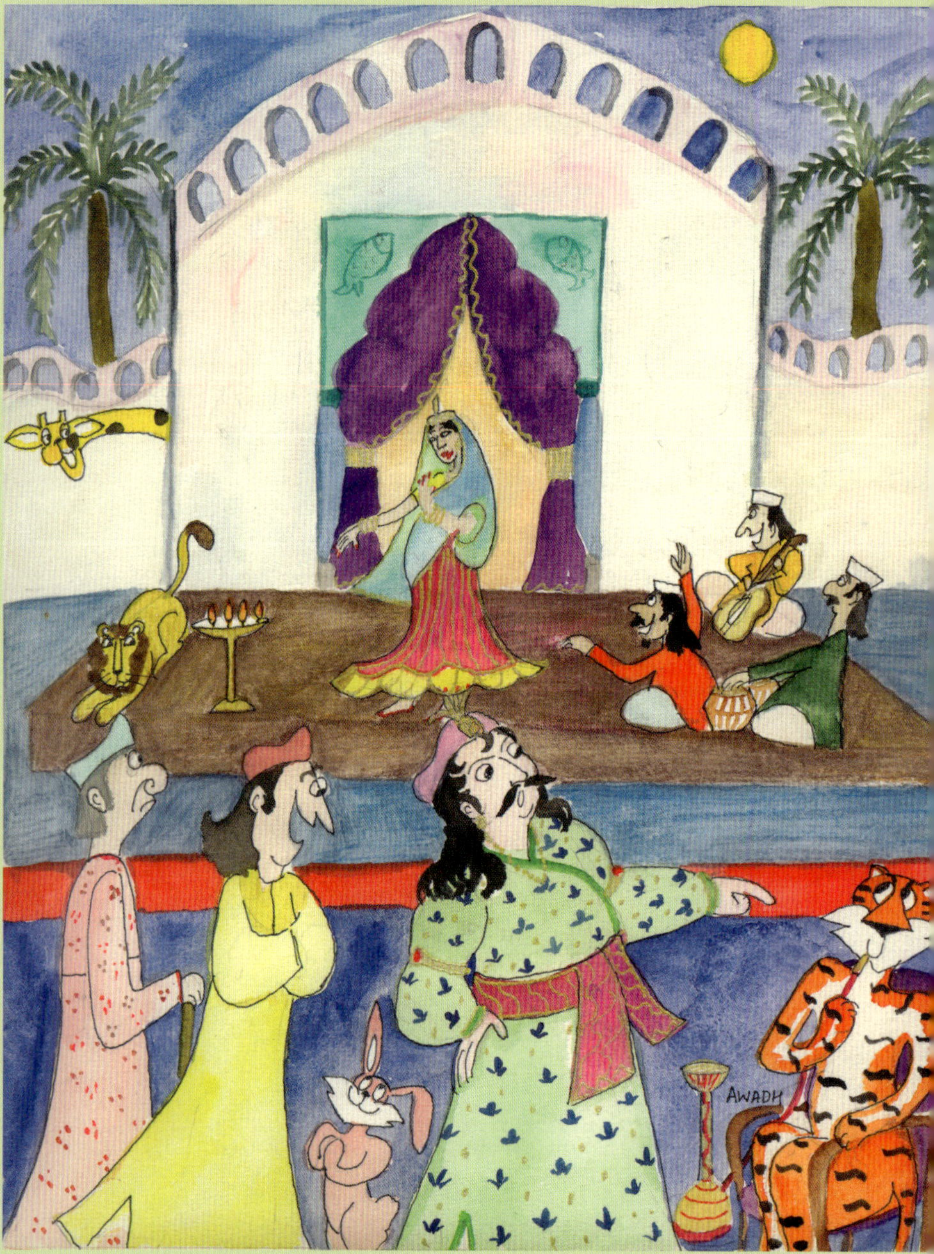
AWADH

There was once a kingdom of Awadh and it was ruled by an aesthete named Wajid Ali Shah (1822-1887) in a land named Hindustan. Lucknow, the capital of the kingdom, as well as of the state of Uttar Pradesh, was famous for its refinement, courtly manners and grace, music and dance, and for the exquisite food prepared by fastidious chefs. The British, like all spoilsports, did not like it. “Decadent”, they called it, and took Wajid Ali Shah as a prisoner to Calcutta.

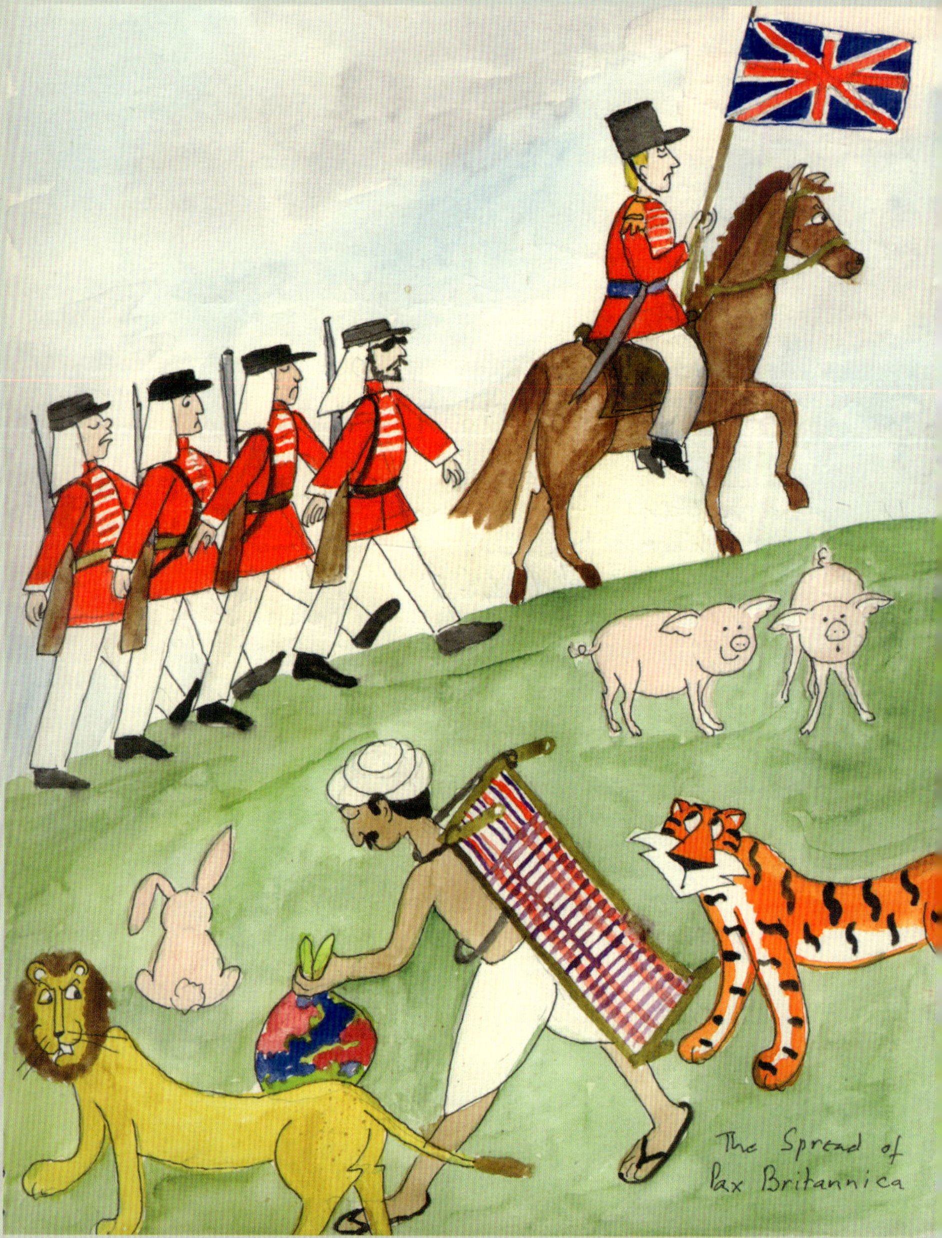
The Spread of
Pax Britannica

Then came the British...

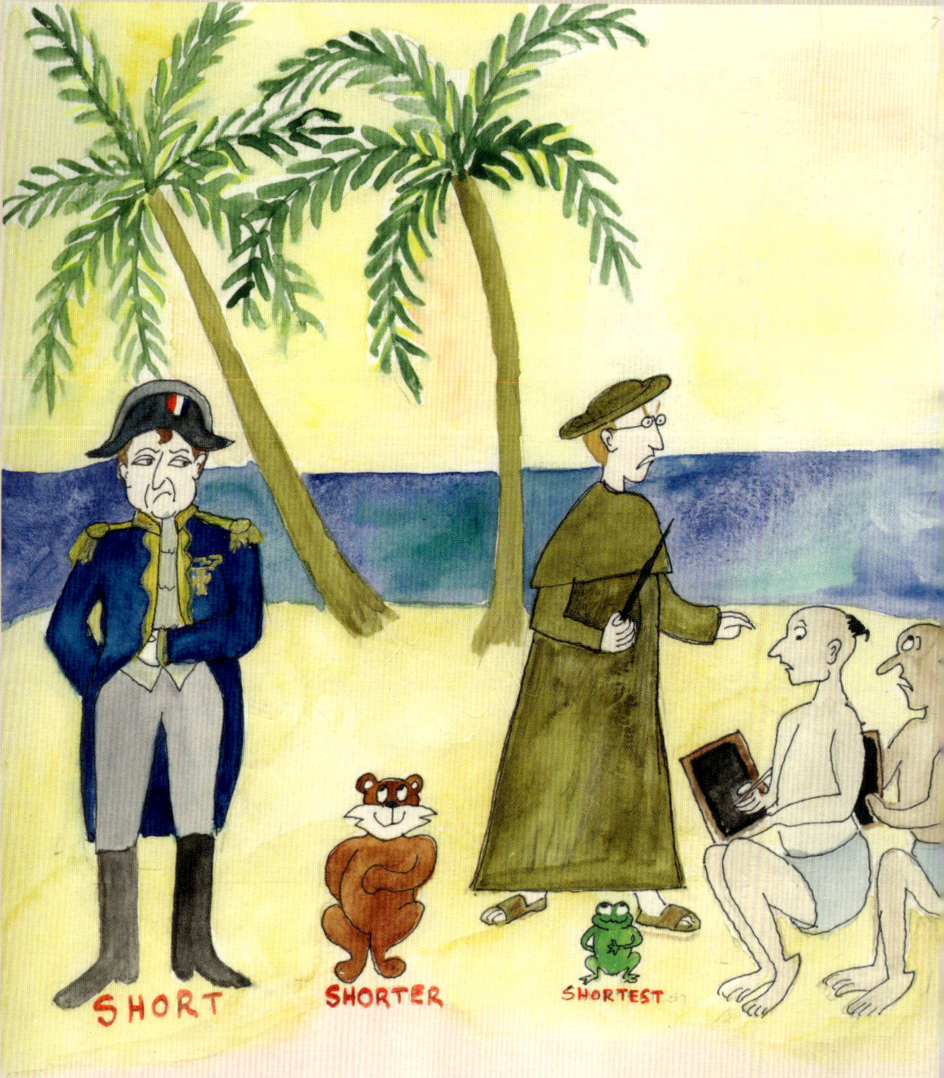

Colonisation

With the British, came Lord Macaulay's Minute on Education of 1835: "We must at present do our best to form a class who may be interpreters between us and the millions whom we govern; a class of persons, Indian in blood and colour, but English in taste, in opinions, in morals, and in intellect." And so the *babus* (clerks) or Macaulay's Children were born. This piece of writing is the greatest in colonial literature.

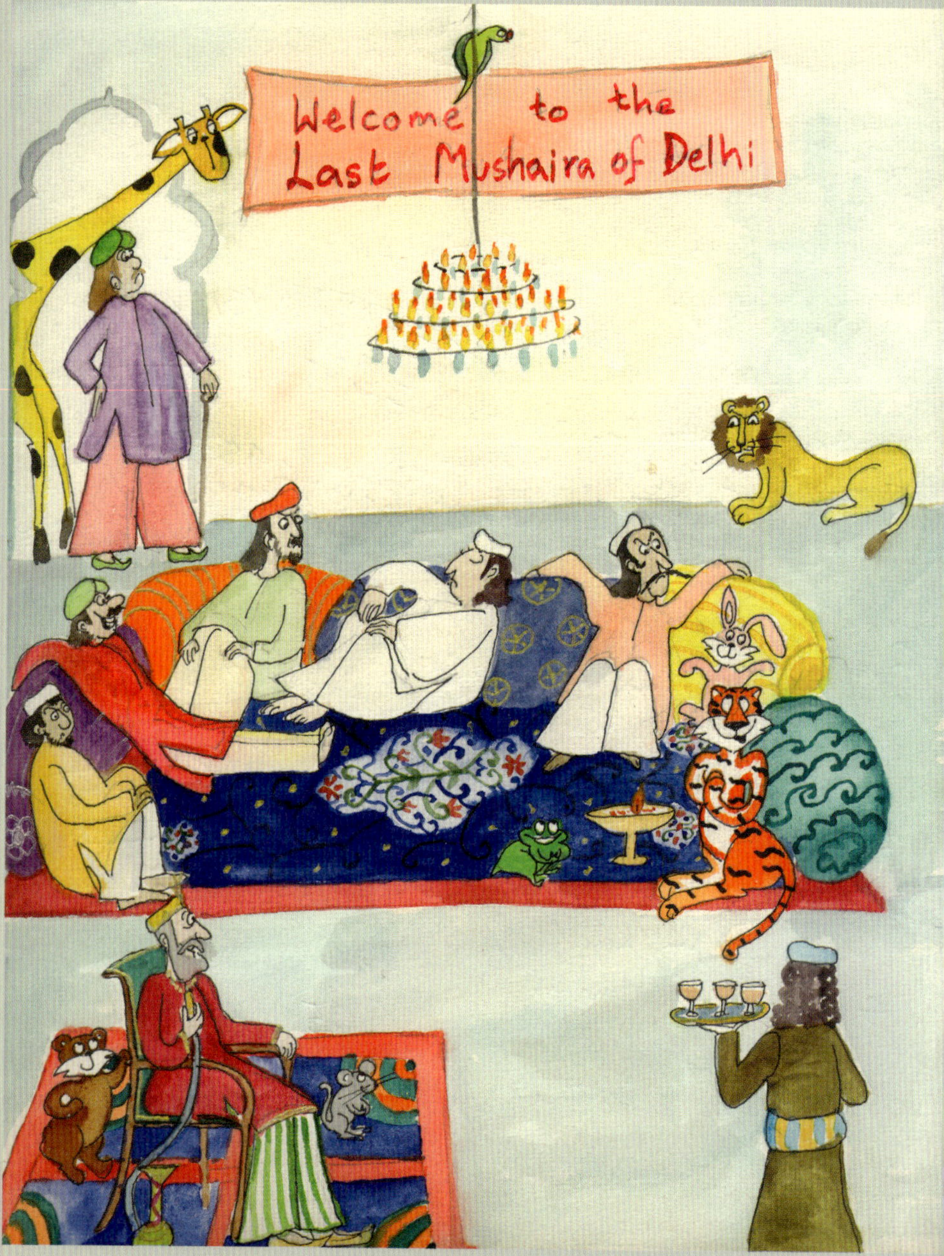
Welcome to the
Last Mushaira of Delhi

And while the Indian way of life, language and culture was being disbanded in favour of an English lifestyle, the Mughals held their last *mushaira* (a gathering of poets) in Delhi (1856) to say goodbye to the *ghazal* and the nightingale...

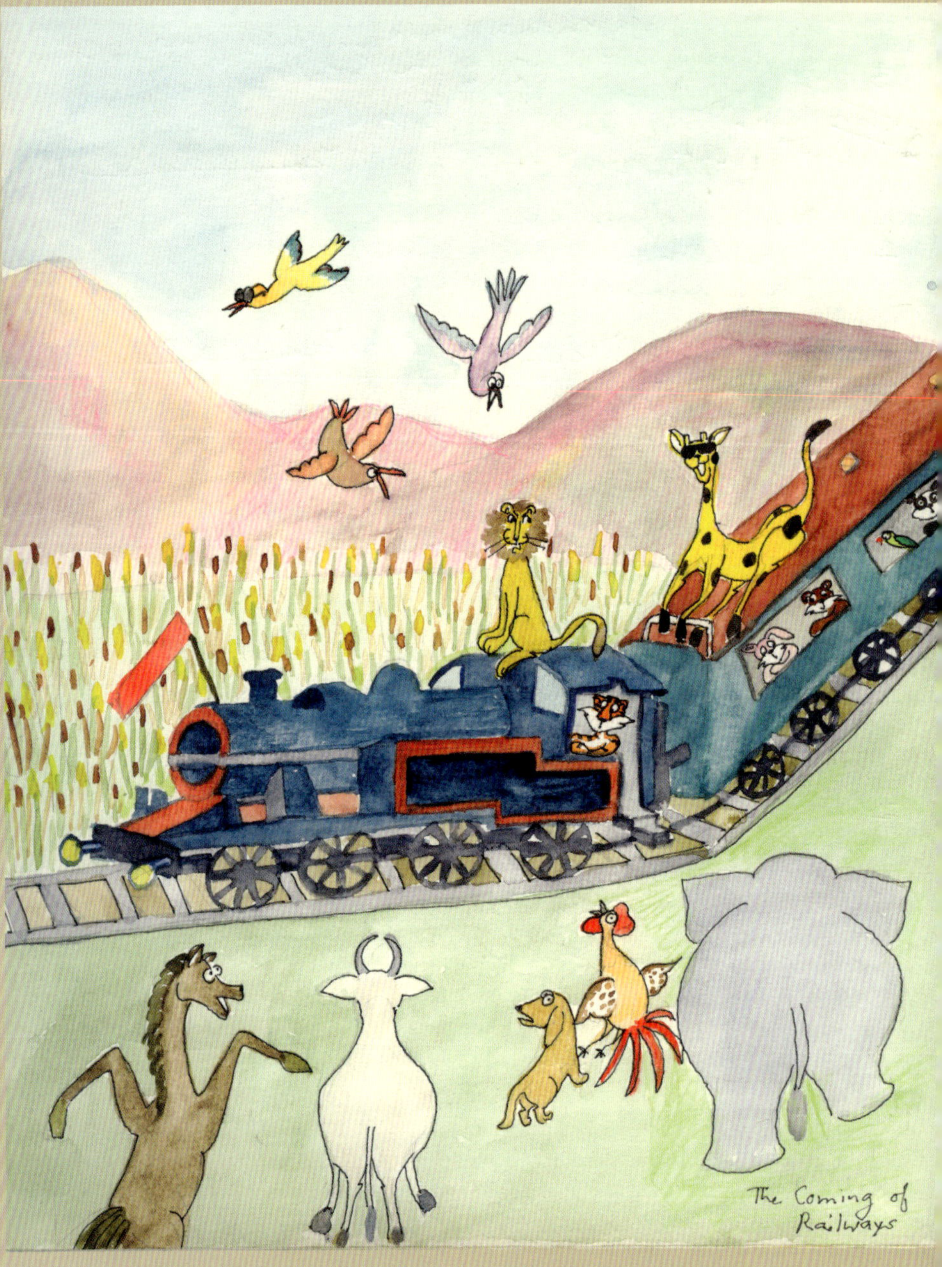
The Coming of Railways

Since 1851, railways were built, criss-crossing the country. The sounds of hurtling engines belching smoke and hooting, traumatised the countryside.

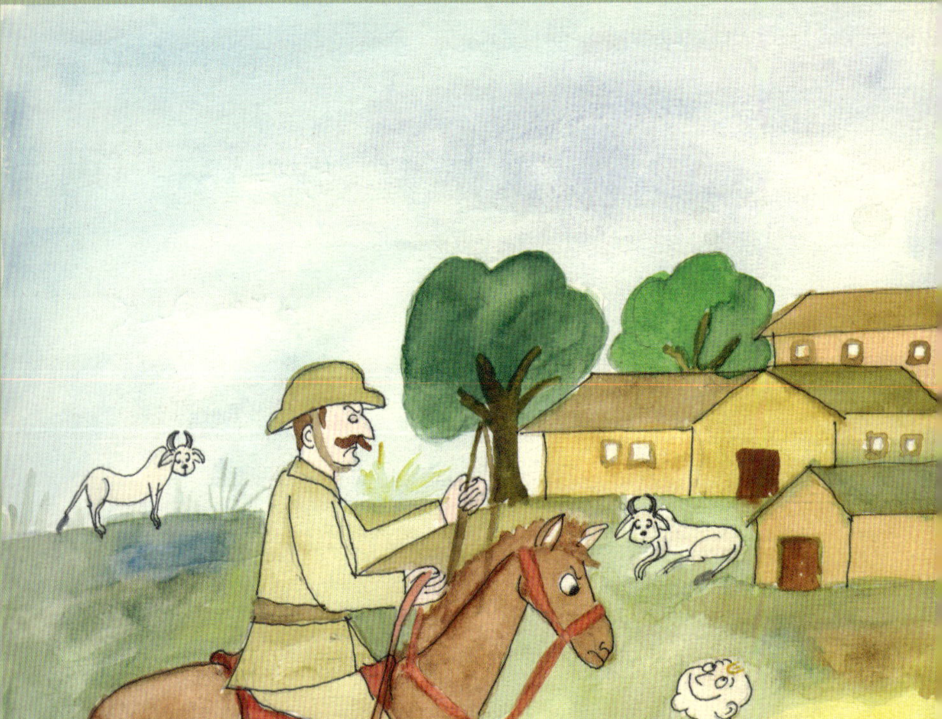
Pax Britannica
and the ICS

The British administered the country with the heaven-born ICS officers who brought justice and succour to the poor peasants. This was known as the *Ma-Baap* (mother-father) regime...

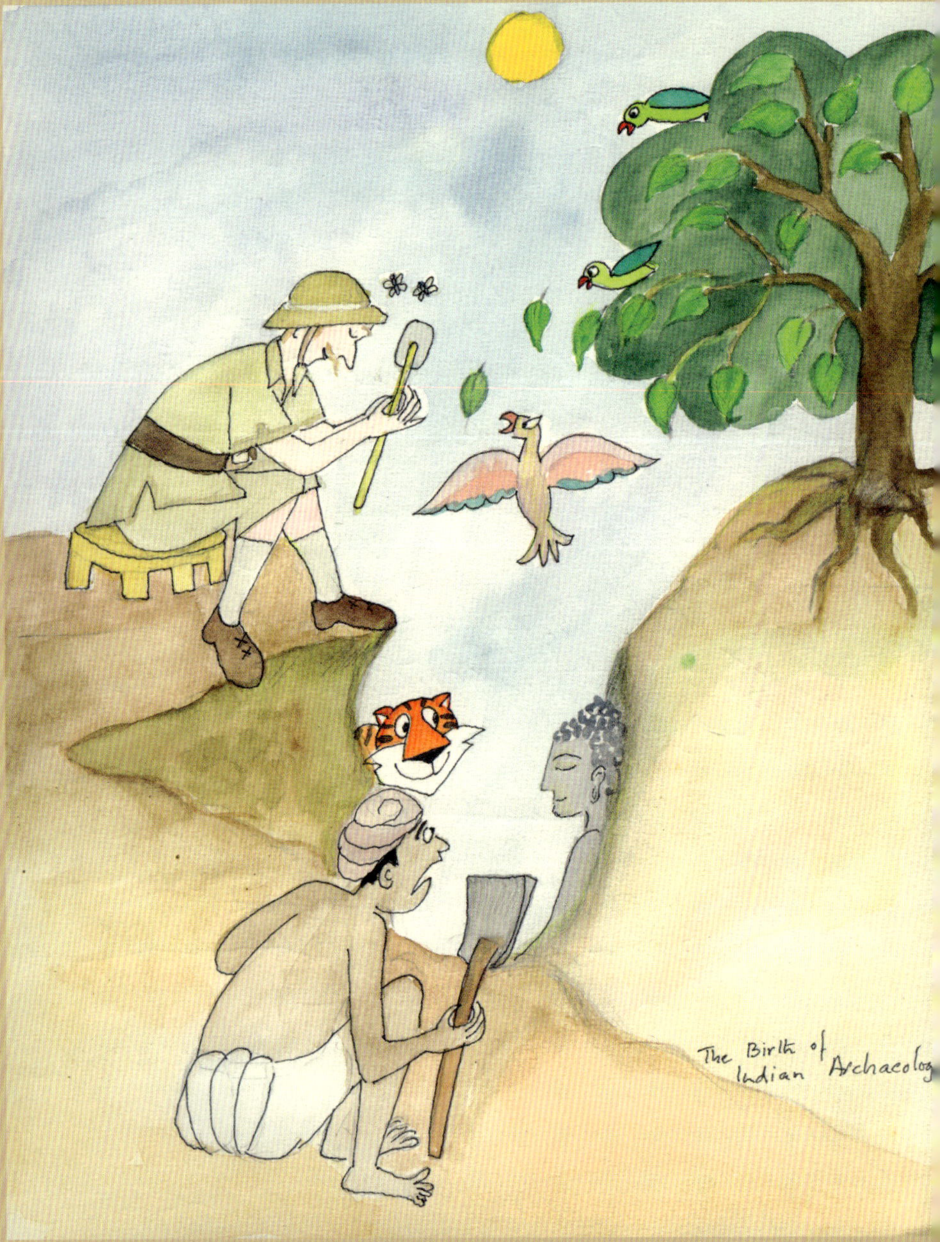
The Birth of Indian Archaeolog

British gentlemen armed with spade and shovel discovered and uncovered India's past and in 1861, the Archaeological Survey of India was founded.

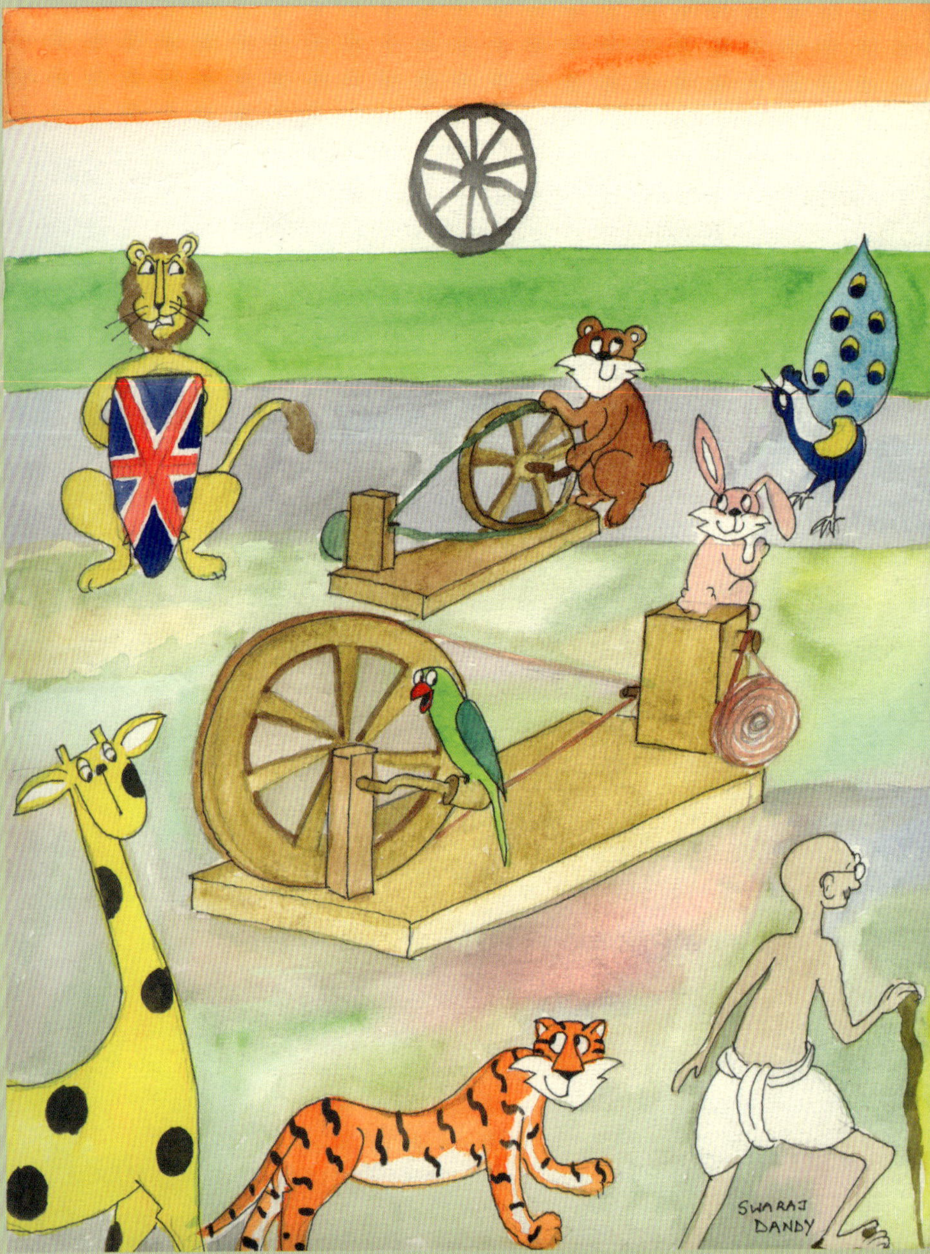
SWARAJ
DANDY

India's struggles for Independence: *Swaraj* or home rule, spinning *khadi* for self-reliance, the Salt Satyagraha of 1930, the start of civil disobedience. That's how a non-violent movement is run...Jai Hind.

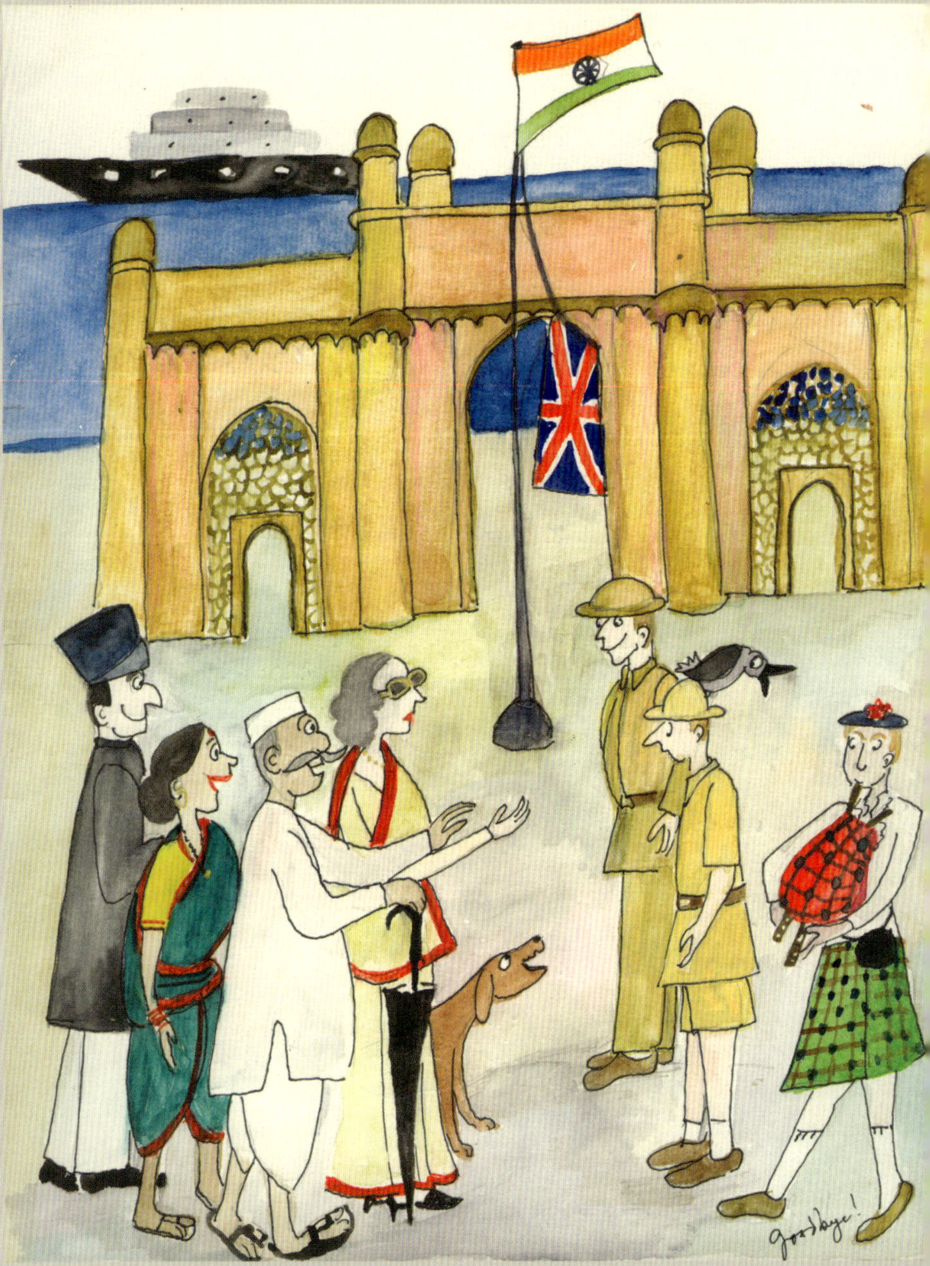
Goodbye!

1947: The British transferred power to a partitioned subcontinent of India and Pakistan. One by one, British battalions left by boat from Mumbai's Gateway to India. It was "Good bye to all that...cheerio..."

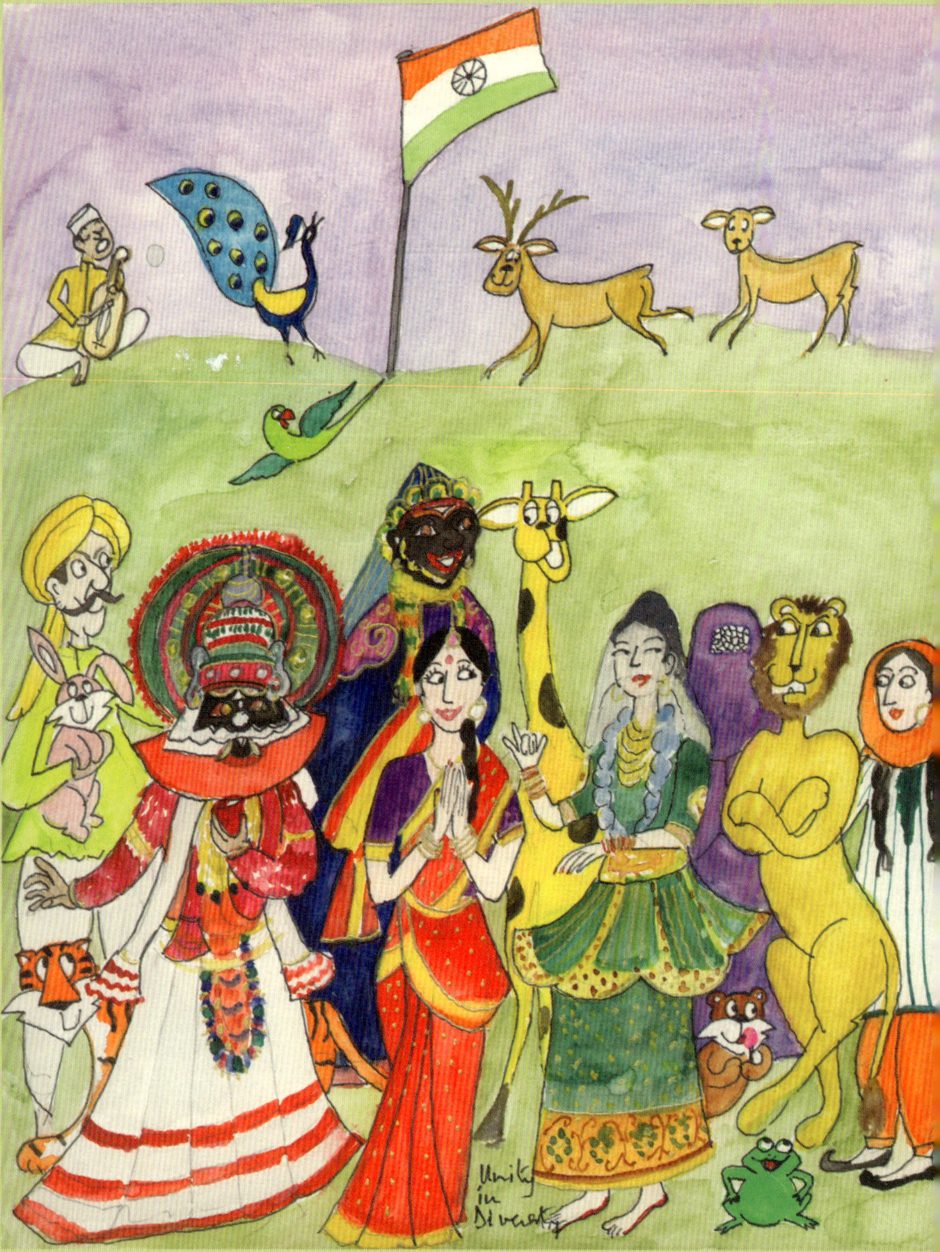
Unity in Diversity

The Indian Constitution came into effect on 26 January 1950 with the resounding words: "We the people (and the animals) of India..."

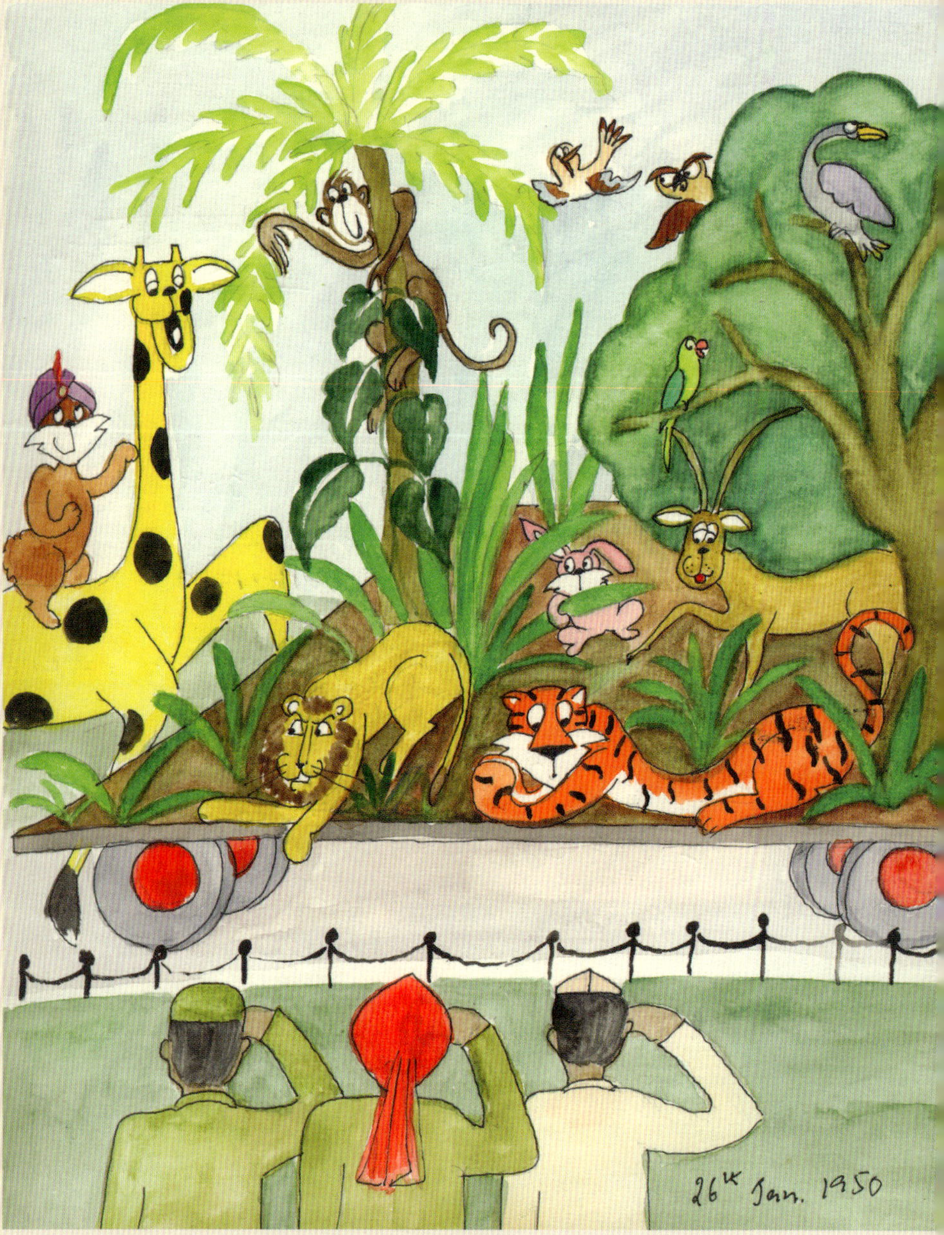
26th Jan. 1950

The first Republic day parade was held on the same day and the opening float was The Indian Jungle. It was wonderful and they were given a standing ovation.

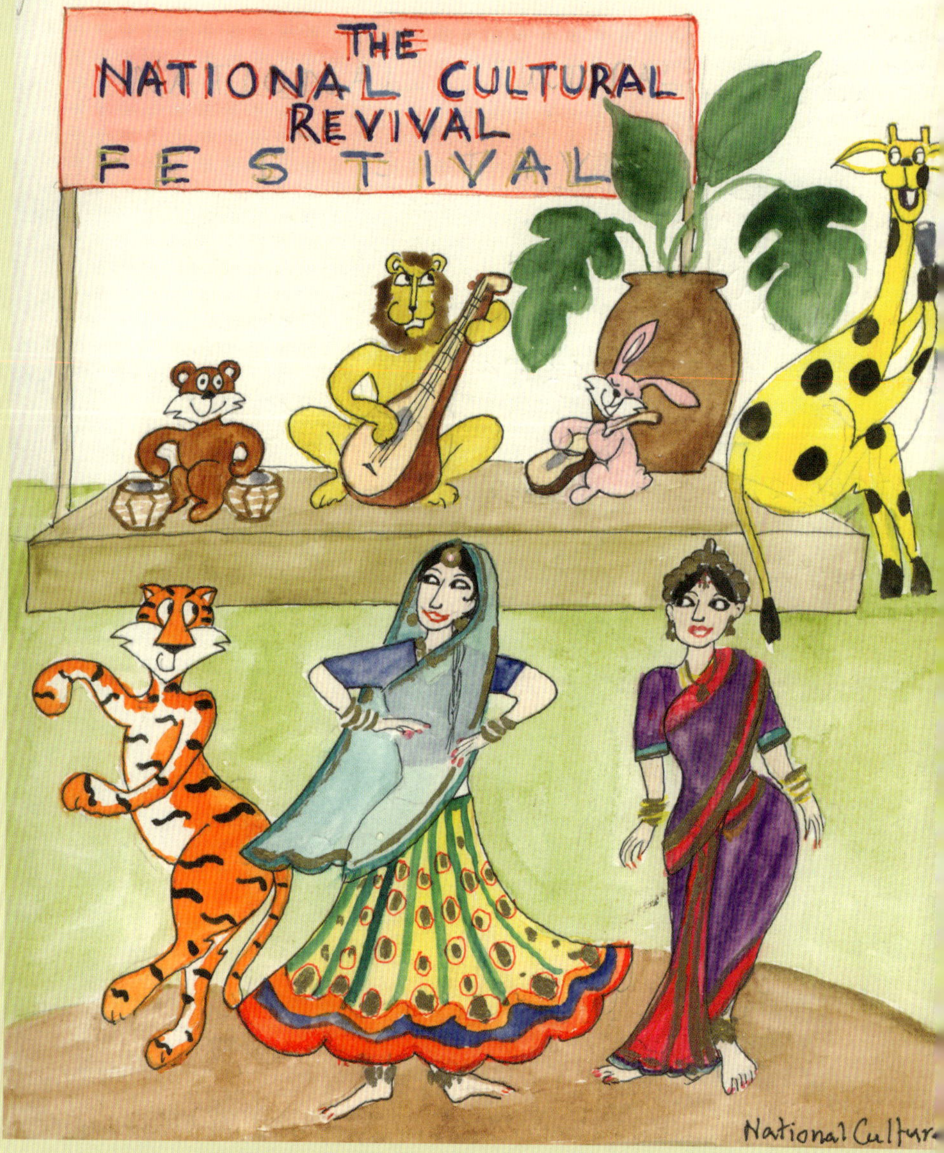
THE
NATIONAL CULTURAL
REVIVAL
FESTIVAL
National Cultur.

1950s: A new nation had to build a national culture and so all the singers and dancers of India came to New Delhi to perform on radio and in the concert halls. We have never looked back and are now suffering from a cultural deluge!

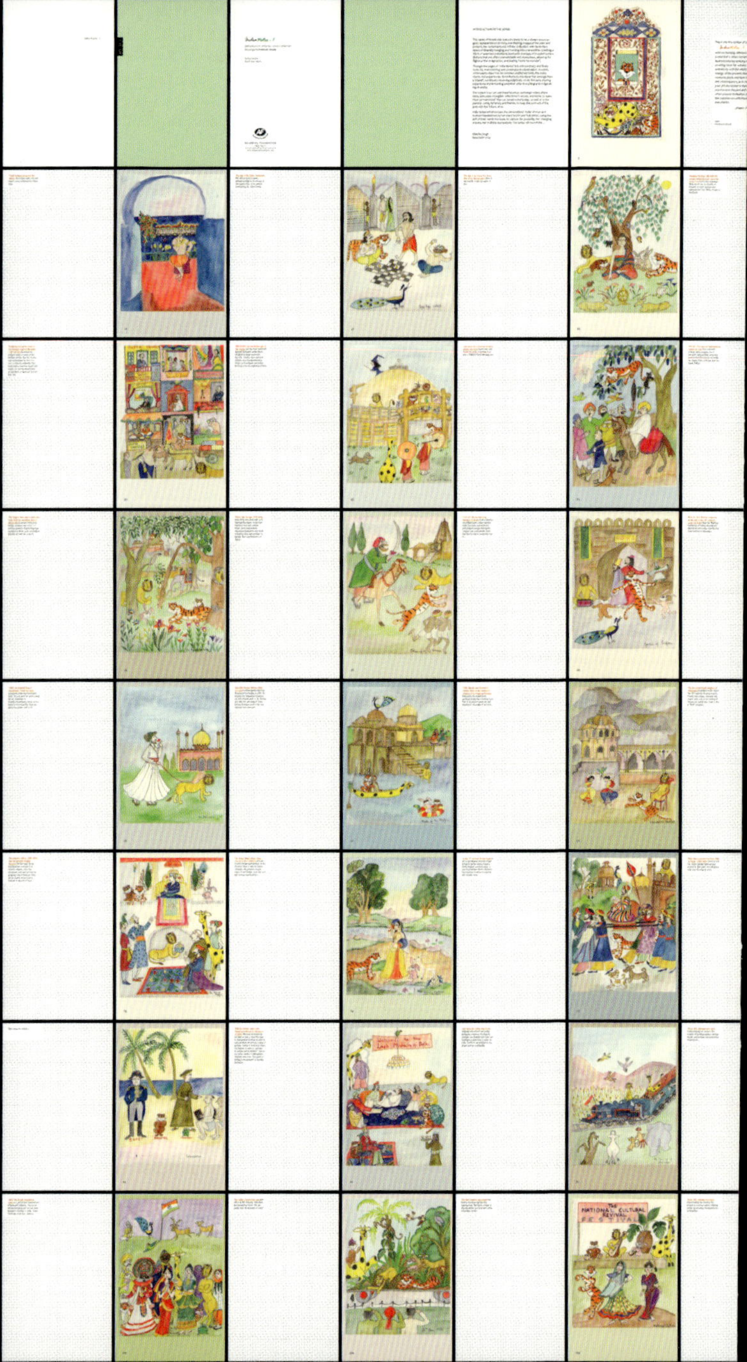

1-14

15-28

29-42

43-56

57-70

71-84

85-98

99-112

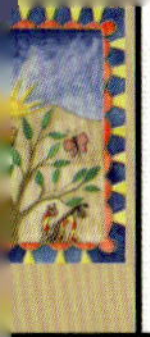
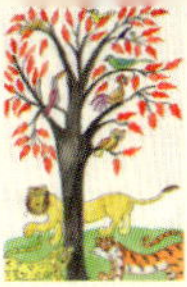
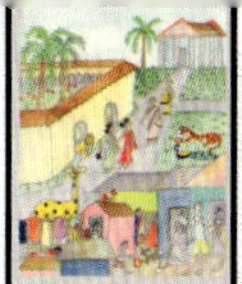
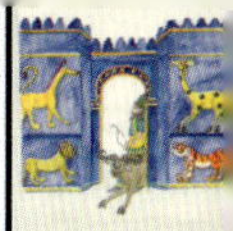
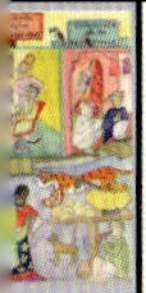
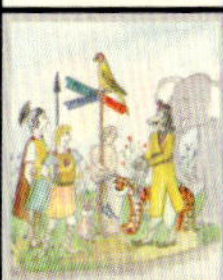
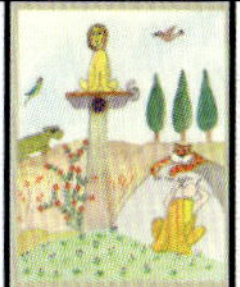
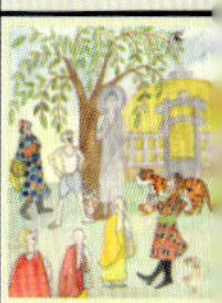
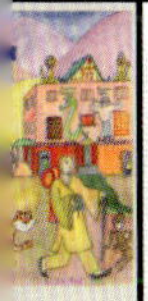
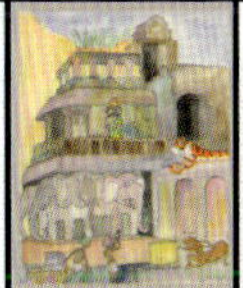
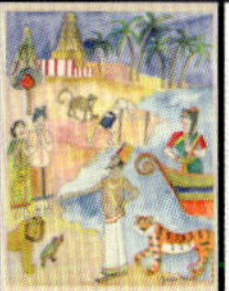
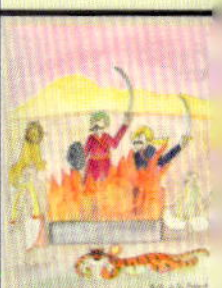
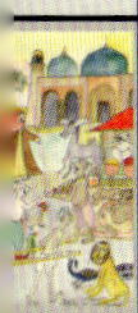
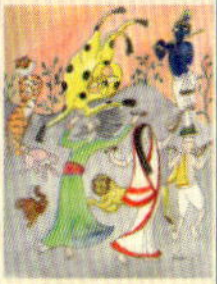
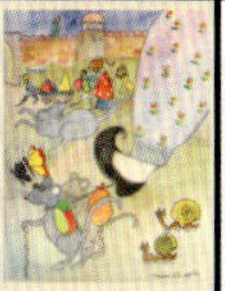
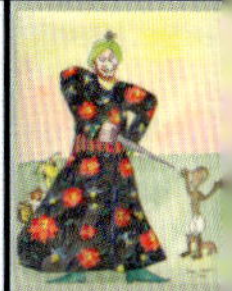
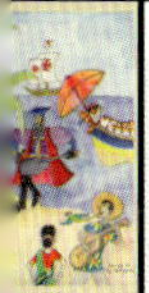
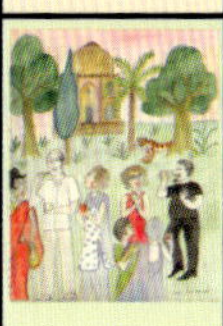
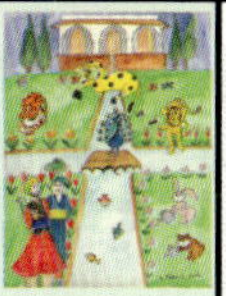
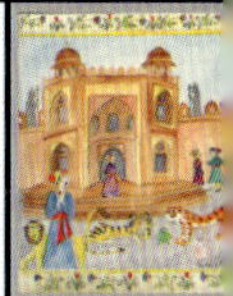
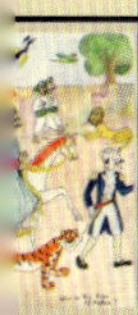
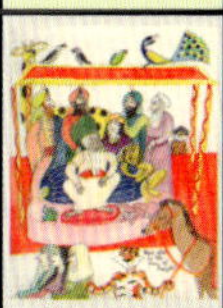
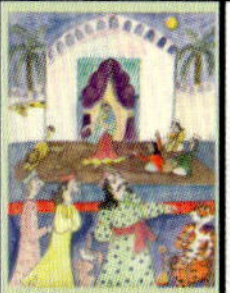
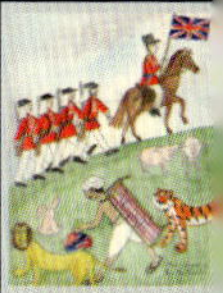
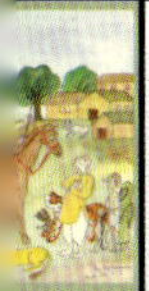
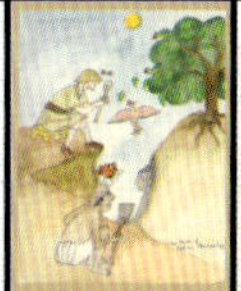
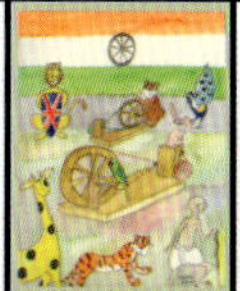
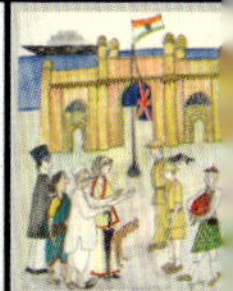
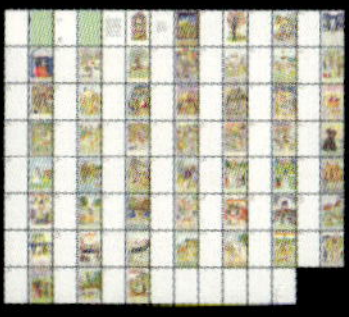

First published in 2015
by
LIMITED EDITIONS
an imprint of

ACADEMIC FOUNDATION

Delhi Sales Office:
4772-73/23 Bharat Ram Road,
(23 Ansari Road), Darya Ganj,
New Delhi - 110 002 (India).
Tel : +91-11-23245001 / 02.
Fax : +91-11-23245005.

Corporate Office:
No. 35, Sector 7,
IMT Manesar,
Gurgaon - 122050.
Haryana (India).
Tel: +91-124-4215070 / 71.

E-mail : books@academicfoundation.com
www.academicfoundation.org

Ageless India, Book 1
Shramana's View of Indian History:
Drawings by Premola Ghose

Series Editor: Malvika Singh

ISBN 13: 9789332702011

Designed, printed and bound by
The Book Mint, New Delhi.
www.thebookmint.in